D1034631

THE ROLEPLAYING GAME OF KAIJU CAPITALISM

WRITING
Rob Wieland

ART
Brian Patterson

DEVELOPMENT
Leonard Balsera • PK Sullivan

EDITING
Karen Twelves

PROOFREADING
Anna Meade

LAYOUT & GRAPHIC DESIGN
Fred Hicks

ART DIRECTION
Brian Patterson

MARKETING
Carrie Harris

CREATIVE DIRECTION
Fred Hicks

PROJECT MANAGEMENT
Sean Nittner • Sophie Lagacé

BUSINESS DEVELOPMENT
Chris Hanrahan

PRODUCT DEVELOPMENT
Fred Hicks • Chris Hanrahan

BASED ON THE CARD GAME BY
Eric B. Vogel

EVIL HAT PRODUCTIONS

An Evil Hat Productions Publication
www.evilhat.com • feedback@evilhat.com
@EvilHatOfficial on Twitter
facebook.com/EvilHatProductions

Kaiju Incorporated: The Roleplaying Game

First published in 2016 by Evil Hat Productions, LLC.
10125 Colesville Rd #318, Silver Spring, MD 20901.

Special thanks to the Fate fans at Nexus Game
Fair and Gamehole Con for game mechanics
feedback and job interview horror stories.

TABLE OF CONTENTS

IT'S NOT JUST AN ADVENTURE, IT'S A JOB

Imagine a world where monsters are real. We're not talking vampires or werewolves, but the giant monsters of B-movie cinema stomping their way through cardboard cities. In this world, giant monster attacks are one more natural disaster, and many famous cities have been rebuilt multiple times. This cyclical process gave rise to a billion dollar industry for the companies that rebuilt the cities, built the machines that fought the monsters, and cleaned up the remains of the creatures. This is the world of **Kaiju Incorporated**.

Companies build the weapons and sell them to the highest bidder, send out crews to clean up the mess made in the battle, carve up the carcasses to sell for research, and then create new, mostly non-dangerous products to sell to the general public. Though lives are endangered whenever a monster attacks and safety standards on K-Tek products are notoriously lacking, the public scrambles for their Kalgon plush dolls and kaijuskin handbags. Big monsters are big business and business is good.

When a kaiju strikes, the corporations call in a kaiju Ace to take the monster down. Aces pilot giant mechanized suits of armor called *batteboto* and duke it out with the monsters in one-on-one combat. Conventional military weapons and tactics rarely handle kaiju well, so a city under attack gets a ringside seat to a battle between man and kaiju.

Aces get all the glory when a kaiju falls. Their public images are part pro wrestler, part war hero, part pro athlete and all spokesperson for their sponsoring corporation. They stop the monster and then fly off into the sunset just in time for a movie premiere or dinner with a head of state.

All the destruction left behind gets handled by **kaiju crews**. These working-class heroes make sure that the insurance paperwork gets filed, the kaiju blood gets mopped up, and that the amateur kaiju hunters and Ace fans don't get hurt trying to get too close to the action. Kaiju Aces get the glory; kaiju crews get the gruntwork. Somebody has to navigate the bureaucracy, hypocrisy, and red tape of the kaiju corporations to make sure that the people truly affected by the attacks get the protection they need. Then it's time to celebrate with a few rounds of drinks at their local tavern while ordering a few dozen pizzas on the corporate credit card.

Kaiju crews are the focus of the *Kaiju Incorporated RPG*. The life of a crew member is plenty exciting. Crews rescue innocent people caught up in the dangerous battles caused by kaiju fighting *batteboto*. They track kaiju to their lairs to capture them, sometimes stopping a kaiju before it unleashes a devastating attack by calling in an preemptive strike. They transport dangerous kaiju materials to secret laboratories—or sometimes steal material from rival companies. They weave through corporate intrigues for the promise of a massive payday or a ticket out of the Bio-Matter Recovery Division. The crew is a family that isn't afraid to crack wise in the face of danger. At Kaiju Incorporated, it's not just an adventure. It's a job.

WHAT'S DIFFERENT FROM FATE CORE?

Here's a summary of the changes from **Fate Core** to the **Kaiju Incorporated RPG**.

Skills: Selecting skills uses a variation on modes as seen in **Fate System Toolkit** and the **Atomic Robo Roleplaying Game**. Any skills above Mediocre are trained; three are focused, and one is specialized.

Aspects: There are five aspects—a high concept, three aspects each connected to one of the selected modes, and one aspect that will come out of a scene from the character's job interview.

Danger Aspects: These are situational aspects created by the table when a kaiju attacks. The bigger the threat the kaiju poses, the more aspects get created. The crew clear these aspects by engaging in contests, challenges, and conflicts.

Stress and Consequences: The game uses one stress track that starts with two stress boxes. If Fitness or Ambition are trained skills, they add one box each, for a range of three to four stress boxes on the average character.

Hybrid Stunts: These more powerful stunts reflect genetic modifications on the character by one of the kaiju corporations. Whenever a character uses a hybrid stunt, instead of paying a fate point, the player whose character is affected by the stunt gains a fate point.

Fate Budget: The GM starts with a number of fate points equal to twice the number of players at the table. These are the fate points she uses to invoke aspects for her characters. Compels feed back into the fate budget (page 52), as do uses of hybrid stunts by the players.

WHAT YOU NEED TO PLAY

- A copy of **Fate Core System**
- **Kaiju Incorporated RPG** character sheets
- A handful of Fate dice (Enough for GM and players, plus some extras for the crisis board. Alternatively you can also use Fate Tokens for your crisis board, available through Campaign Coins at *http://campaigncoins.com/coins/fate/*.)
- Sticky notes or index cards
- Crisis board, created by laying out sticky notes or index cards out on the table (For maximum corporate synergy, a dry-erase whiteboard will prove useful.)
- Gold star stickers (Optional but fun!)
- A copy of the card game **Kaiju Incorporated** (Optional but awesome for inspiration and fun illustrations, available at *http://www.evilhat.com.*)

Q&K An Interview With Kerri "Wooz" Woosley, Kaiju Crew Shift Captain

This month's *Footprint Magazine* profile isn't the usual glamorous story told in a penthouse overlooking Central Park West or the designer sterility of a kaiju corporation conference room. We've profiled the executives leading the kaiju corporations and the scientists pushing the edges of K-Tek research, but we've rarely gotten direct access to one of the crew members that cleans up all the messes made during a kaiju attack. These "kaiju crews" are the bridge between the chaos of a kaiju attack and the order of a normal life.

Kerri Woosley is a middle-aged woman with tired eyes and a warm face. Her rank as Shift Captain is only denoted by the slightly higher cube walls that surround where our interview takes place. She wears a recently laundered jumpsuit that still has the ghost of a stain or two near the elbows and knees. The KleanKrewe logo is everywhere; on her jumpsuit, the coffee mugs, and even the picture frame on her desk that encases a picture of her family. It's a striking contrast to the expensive suits and crisp lab coats seen in other parts of the Kaijumoto Keiretsu building. This part of the building still holds to the decor of the upper floors, but looks like it hasn't been updated beyond a new coat of paint ever since Dr. Kaneda was wandering the halls.

After a big hug and an insistence I call her Wooz, I sit down at a metal desk that looks older than the two of us combined.

FM: Where did you get your nickname?

Wooz: Everyone in the crew gets a nickname. That's when you know you really belong. This is a job with long hours doing things that need to get done but that people don't want to do. You want a name that can be heard on the radio clearly or over a kaiju running at full speed. Most folks should run away from a kaiju attack. Not us. We got things to do.

FM: How did you end up on a kaiju crew?

Wooz: My husband ran a contracting company that folded when the housing market crashed. It was a hell of a thing. All those buildings being rebuilt and rebuilt after kaiju attacks and then people decided they couldn't afford it any more. He got a few construction jobs here and there but I needed to find work to pick up the slack. I really only applied because they were offering daycare right here in the building. Now I make the money and Kyle stays home with the kids. Sometimes I think his job is more dangerous (laughs).

FM: Are your kids afraid you won't come home from a call?

Wooz: Only when we get pulled into a Red Alert and I have to travel. They think it's cool when Mom has to go up in the KreweKopter, but they also know that means I'm running headfirst into danger. The money is good but it's hard for the kids to see a devastated city and not think Mom's going to drown in a pool of glowing goop or something. My oldest asked me to come talk to their class. I brought some of the tools we use to show off.

FM: What was their favorite?

Wooz: The kids love the Mjolnir Mittens. They're made from the same material as Thorzilla's skin. Palms open, they deliver a jolt that can restart a battery or even a heart. Palm closed, it can put a looter on their backside if you catch them with a right hook. Oh dear, I probably shouldn't have said that. It's not in the training manual. But it was the first thing my old supervisor told me when I started working here. Saved my backside when I was in Mexico City during Gyros's last attack.

FM: Was that a typical day on the job for you?

Wooz: A typical day is filling out paperwork from the last alert or, if you're lucky, getting a head start on the paperwork for the next one. Alerts come often, but a lot of them are about keeping tabs on kaiju instead of the big dramatic attacks. Mexico City was rough because Gyros's winds caused a lot of property damage. We needed to clear buildings that weren't structurally sound. When *Artemis Heart* went down, our crew got a call to extract the Ace. I stayed behind to finish clearing the damaged building and found some scavengers looking for kaiju leave behinds.

FM: Are you often deployed to active kaiju attacks?

Wooz: We're usually not in the direct path of the kaiju but some Aces don't care much about big brawls all over the place. They're supposed to contain the kaiju but some of them see it as an opportunity to rack up more sponsorship deals if they get flashy. I usually try to get the Ace's name because that can tell you a lot about if you're going to just be dealing with the kaiju or if the batteboto is going to be trying to step on you too.

A light starts flashing above her desk—a Yellow Alert, which means she needs to shuffle me out of the office and get a crew ready to go. On the way out, I mention one last thing.

FM: You still didn't answer my first question.

Wooz: Oh jeez, okay. Six months in, we get a call to Atlanta. Mothballara wedged a city bus onto the eighth floor of the building, and as soon as we've evacuated everyone off the bus, it goes crashing into the street below. A local news crew was on the scene and interviewed me about the rescue operation. I was so excited about it that I told everyone I knew to tune into the six o'clock news to watch them replay the interview. But they misspelled my name—with a "z" instead of an "s." The crew got such a kick out of it that the name stuck. At least I've been on TV.

THE CREWS

It's time to fill out some paperwork and join a crew. Your characters might not have qualified to be Aces or perhaps they landed the job because Uncle Steve works for R&D, but you fulfill a vital role in the world of asset acquisition and kaiju product development!

CREW CREATION CHECKLIST

Discuss Your Ideas: Decide what type of crew you want to be and what role everyone's character fills.

Choose Your Modes: Select one mode at Good (+3), one at Fair (+2), and one at Average (+1). The available modes are Crisis, Lab, Office, and PR.

Focus, Specialization, and Stress: From each of the modes you've selected, choose one skill to focus. Then choose a focused skill to specialize. Add stress boxes if Fitness and Ambition are trained.

Choose Your Aspects: Each character has five aspects. Choose your high concept and mode aspects, and keep your interview aspect blank for now.

Choose Your Stunts: Choose up to three stunts for free and three more by spending refresh. Hybrid stunts offer more powerful effects at the cost of giving the GM more fate points.

The Final Interview: The GM will have a short scene with each character from their initial job interview. Based on how that scene plays out, decide what would be an appropriate fifth aspect for your character.

STEP ONE: DISCUSS YOUR IDEAS

Make sure that everyone is on the same page with the type of crew your table wants to run. It's easy to assume you're going to be a corporate crew, but that's not the only option. Discussing what role you might fill in a kaiju attack will also be helpful at this point.

Kaiju Crew Concepts

Corporate Crew: Well-funded kaiju first responders that have to battle bureaucracy and corporate scheming when not out in the field rescuing people.

Freelance Crew: Independent contractors looking to break into the big leagues while dealing with outdated equipment and dangerous contracts.

Black Market Crew: Illegal scavengers picking off the choicest selections of kaiju remains for sale through illegal channels, often fighting off other criminals for the best bits.

Undercover Crew: Government operatives using the chaos and terror of a kaiju attack to advance the agenda of their shadowy masters.

Rubble Rousers: Amateur kaiju chasers that want to see the big monster up close, even at the risk of interfering with the kaiju crews there to help.

STEP TWO: CHOOSE YOUR MODES

Choose three of the following modes. One is rated at Good (+3), one is rated at Fair (+2), and one is rated at Average (+1). All the skills within each mode have the same rating.

Crisis Mode

Things can get a little hairy out in the field. Even Green and Blue Alerts can bring crew members into contact with belligerent Aces, rival crews, or frightened civilians. Crew members with **Crisis mode** thrive under the pressure that outrunning a hundred-meter-tall mutant aardvark brings to the workplace.

Combat

You're unlikely to go toe-to-toe with a kaiju, but knowing how to handle yourself during an alert is never a bad idea. This skill covers armed and unarmed combat. Combat specialists should look to stunts to illustrate their particular set of skills.

 Create Advantage: This covers all those special moves that characters want to do instead of just punching. If you want to DISARM someone, put them in a HEADLOCK, or even KNEECAP them to get them to talk, roll Combat in this way.

 Attack: If you want to inflict stress on someone with a weapon, this is the skill to use.

Defend: Use Combat to defend against armed and unarmed attacks. For ranged attacks, defend with Fitness.

Fitness

There's a lot of physical activity going on during a kaiju attack. Crew members often have to jump across crumbling rooftops, dodge falling concrete, and try to not get stepped on at least once a week. It's a rating of your general physical fortitude and affects how much stress you can take before you give up.

 Overcome: This covers running, jumping, climbing, or anything you'd see in a non-contact sport.

Create Advantage: You can use this skill to create advantages around maneuvering. That includes getting someone BACKED INTO A CORNER, climbing a wall to GET A BETTER VIEW, or even outrunning a kaiju to TIRE THE MONSTER OUT.

 Defend: Use Fitness to defend against ranged attacks. For close attacks, defend with Combat.

Tradecraft

Sometimes crew members need to get into places where they aren't technically allowed. Tradecraft involves sneaking around, breaking and entering, and getting out with the information needed to catch a kaiju before it becomes a problem.

Overcome: You want to get inside somewhere without being noticed. This includes sneaking past guards in a rival corporation's lab or quietly finding the best route out of a sleeping kaiju's lair.

Create Advantage: Advantages created by this skill often take the form of cobbling together solutions from whatever's at hand, like Makeshift Kaiju Bait or a One-Shot Bazooka Made Out Of Cleaning Supplies.

Lab Mode

If you want your character to know the ins and outs of how the corporations run, you need to understand their technology. **Lab mode** is for characters who like to have the office to themselves, far away from the beasts running rampant in the outside world.

Kaiju Studies

Kaiju have been part of the world for fifty years. There's a lot of data to wade through, but the right info can mean the difference between stopping a kaiju before it trashes a city and getting hauled into the field to scoop waste samples by hand. Characters might not know everything about every kaiju with this skill, but they do know where they can find those crucial bits of info when they are needed.

Overcome: Attempt to understand an unfamiliar kaiju and what its strengths and weaknesses might be. For example, knowing if ingesting raw kaiju meat is poisonous when hard up for supplies.

Create Advantage: Make useful bits of trivia that crews can use for their own survival. Knowing that MOTHBALLARA ALWAYS ATTACKS AT SUNRISE gives crews time to prepare. If AMANDA LIKES THE SCENT OF LAVENDER, the crew can rig up some massive diffusers to lure her into a trap.

Technology

The world is full of high technology. This skill unlocks cell phones, tracks radio signals, and lets the crew member use modern conveniences to the best of their capabilities. This skill also covers the weird world of K-Tek devices.

Overcome: This skill covers most elements of what the public would call hacking when it comes to computer security. It also lets you use a K-Tek device without reading the manual or even knowing which end to point at the kaiju before pressing the button.

Create Advantage: Technology makes life easier and advantages created with this skill often make follow-ups that help other skills. If you DOWNLOADED THE BOSS'S HARD DRIVE, you can get a leg up on salary negotiations. It can also represent small K-Tek devices your character has on their person, like ANTI-PHEREMONE GUM or ANGINUS CLIMBING PADS.

Operate

Whether it's a helicopter circling a rampaging Mothballara, a bulldozer fleeing a crumbling industrial park, or a delivery van full of Gatcha Pizza, there are a lot of things that can be driven, piloted, and otherwise operated to get your character from one place to another.

 Overcome: Use this to overcome bad terrain or when a vehicle needs precise control to avoid taking damage.

 Create Advantage: Vehicles often allow for excellent advantages like TARGET LOCKS or fancy moves like DRIFTING BEHIND YOU.

 Attack: If you want to inflict physical stress while behind the stick, use this skill.

 Defend: You can swerve out of the way to avoid physical stress with this skill.

Skill Flexibility

We've called out the most common uses of each skill in these write-ups. Uses outside these actions are atypical, but Fate GMs sometimes allow a bit of flexibility, depending on how well-rounded their protagonists should feel. If you want skills to work outside the actions listed in the descriptions, we've included suggestions below on how to make this happen. Make sure to communicate about which option you choose with your group.

Stunts: Substitution stunts are a common solution to this issue. Spend a stunt slot to use a higher skill in a specific situation with the right action. This is probably the strictest of these variations, since it locks in a specific deviation when the fiction fits.

Declaration: If an aspect is judged to be useful in a particular situation, consider allowing a player to use a skill to perform an action that might not normally be used. This allows justification at the cost of fate points, which means players are paying a cost to bend the rules. But it also means players are more likely to justify aspect spends to try and break the rules.

Situational: If the fiction fits, the player can use the skill for a different action *without* spending fate points. This is the most powerful variation, since it offers players a chance to have characters using their best skills nearly all the time. It also can inspire a bit of negotiation between the player and the GM as to whether the skill applies. Constant negotiations can slow down play, however.

Office Mode

Crew members would like to think that they are out of danger at the office. In most kaiju corporations, intrigue and politics reign supreme. It takes more than a sense of direction to roam the carpeted halls and cubicle walls. It takes cunning, charm, and a desire to know just how much money everybody makes. **Office mode** covers all these skills.

Ambition

A character with this skill has the drive to succeed and the will to stand tall when others have thrown in the towel. It keeps you awake in useless meetings and lets you figure out what the home office meant in its garbled text. It's a rating of your general mental fortitude and affects how much stress you can take before you give up.

Overcome: This skill overcomes mental challenges like puzzles and riddles. It is also a component of kaiju-related challenges and contests, because facing down a giant monster can be absolutely terrifying.

Defend: Ambition is used to defend against Provoke attacks and other mind-control attempts. If it is in a trained mode, it gives you an additional stress box.

Networking

As is often the case in the corporate world, crew members may have gotten their jobs through friends, co-workers, and other relationships. This skill represents how well you maintain those relationships and, more importantly, how you use them to your advantage.

Overcome: This skill represents the legwork you can do to gain information. You talk to your friends and they tell you what they know. It can also be used to seek out a hard-to-reach person, like an executive or government official, but that person might not always be available to dispense further information.

Create Advantage: Networking can also be used to create and cash in favors from your contacts. You can create advantages to represent how a KAIJU ACE OWES YOU ONE or how DANNY IN MARKETING THINKS YOU'RE CUTE.

Defend: Use this skill to defend against others trying to inflict stress on you by spreading rumors and ruining your relationships.

Rapport

Characters that want to get people on their side use this skill. It reflects sincerity but it's not just for honest people. People can still be manipulative when they aren't flat out lying.

Overcome: This skill is often used in contests, which makes it useful in a crisis when trying to get someone else to do something for you. It can also be used as a quick way to resolve a social interaction without diving into a contest.

Create Advantage: You can use this skill to create advantages based on your ability to connect with people. THE CROWD IS ON YOUR SIDE makes public appeals easier, while THE JUDGE BELIEVES YOU can make winning a social contest far easier to win.

Defend: Good Rapport can defend against mental stress inflicted by Provoke, so long as it's just words and not physical bullying.

PR Mode

PR mode is most often chosen by outgoing characters. Characters with this mode feel at ease when the cameras are on them and they're being asked questions at the press conference. This mode isn't about careful diplomacy; it's about making a quick emotional attachment that can be exploited for personal gain later.

Empathy

Empathy reflects your ability to judge people and their emotional states. If you know what they're feeling, you know how you can help. You also know what to say to get them to do what you want.

Overcome: The Good Cop approach. Point out similarities or tell stories to someone and they're more likely to share information. It also lets you remove mental consequences when you take some time talking things out over a cup of coffee.

Create Advantage: Understanding emotional states makes it easy to generate sympathy. When you tell someone You Know How They Feel, they are more likely to open up and come out with a positive perspective of you.

Defend: Often used to defend against Spin attempts to perceive the truth of the matter.

Provoke

You know just what to say to hurt people. Not everyone reacts the same to honeyed words. Sometimes you've got to squirt a little vinegar in their eye to get them to act.

Overcome: The Bad Cop approach. You can scare someone into getting what you want. If it's not worth naming the target, one roll is often all it takes.

Create Advantage: Threaten something near and dear to a person and you're likely to get them to do what you want. Knowing Their Job Is on the Line or that You Know Where They Live can get resistant people to open up. If someone holds out on you, you might have to inflict stress on them in a mental conflict to get them to talk, which leads to our next option below.

Attack: This skill can cause stress when applied to targets unwilling to budge. Enough mental stress from yelling or cutting insults can get an opponent to make a mistake or open up to consequences.

Spin

Lies are an important part of a corporate breakfast. Company spokespeople even lie about what they call lies. This skill lets you convincingly tell people what they want to believe instead of the truth. If they don't call you out on it, it's not your fault.

Overcome: When you want to bluff your way through a bad situation, this is the skill to use. You can always apologize later if you need to feel better about yourself.

Create Advantage: When you know the truth and they don't, you have an advantage. This can mean something like A GOOD COVER STORY when trying to get inside a secure area, or FAKING AN INJURY to throw off an opponent in a contest.

Defend: You can misdirect people who use Empathy to see who you really are. You choose who sees that. Nobody else.

Dude, Where's My Notice Skill?

Notice's usual sphere of "Is there anything unusual here?" is covered by skills related to that purpose. Any skill that has an overcome action can also be used to notice any strangeness related to that skill. Tradecraft can detect when a crime scene has been disturbed, while Empathy can tell when the secretary has been crying. Notice's abilities for determining who goes when in a conflict have been split between Fitness for physical conflicts and Ambition for mental conflicts.

STEP THREE:
MODIFY SKILLS AND STRESS

Once you've chosen your three modes, look at the three skills inside each mode. Those skills are considered **trained** at the level you chose for the mode. All three skills in your Good mode start at +3, all the skills in the Fair mode are at +2, and all the skills in Average mode are +1.

Choose one skill in each of the three modes you've selected. Your character has received additional training and development in those skills. Add +1 to their current rank. These skills are considered **focused**.

Of the three focused skills your character has, choose one. That skill gains another rank and is considered **specialized**. The specialized skill should be two ranks above the other skills in the mode. For example, if you trained Tradecraft at Good (+3), then focused it to Great (+4), you could specialize it to Superb (+5).

Characters begin with two stress boxes and three consequence slots. Anyone with Fitness or Ambition as a trained skill gains an extra stress box. If both Fitness and Ambition are trained, gain two stress boxes.

STEP FOUR: CHOOSE YOUR ASPECTS

Once you've chosen your modes, it's time to choose aspects for your character. Choose four aspects for your character now—your high concept (if you haven't already) and one aspect for each of the modes your character possesses. The fifth aspect will be chosen during the interview phase. We've also added **hybrid aspects**, which embrace the B-movie roots of the genre by adding the powers of the kaiju directly to your character (page 24).

High Concept Aspect

Your **high concept** is a short summary of your character concept in a few words. There's some excellent advice for making these in **Fate Core**, but if all else fails, take a noun, add an interesting adjective in front of it, and you're good to go! Feel free to mix and match the words in the list below when inspiration is lacking. A DISCREDITED JANITOR and a SARCASTIC SPY have wildly different stories to tell. While other aspects have space to be a little more flowery, the more straightforward this aspect is, the more flexible and useful you will find it to be.

High Concept Aspects

DISCREDITED ACADEMIC

RELUCTANT SPY

HAUNTED SOLDIER

BRILLIANT JANITOR

SARCASTIC PILOT

ALPHA INTERN

SHY BUREAUCRAT

SLOW CON ARTIST

DELIBERATE SCIENTIST

UNLIKELY SPOKESPERSON

Crisis Mode Aspects

Your Crisis mode aspect reflects your first instincts when things go to hell. Are you worried about yourself or others? Do you charge toward danger or away from it? Do you lead from the front or from the back? Aspects affect your overall character, but this one will be most useful whenever it's time to throw a little action into the game.

Crisis Mode Aspects

ADRENALINE JUNKIE

FIND A HOLE TO HIDE IN
    AND STAY THERE

PROTECT THE INNOCENT

FORMER KAIJU ACE

ALWAYS CALL FOR BACKUP

NEVER CALL FOR BACKUP

NO GUTS, NO GLORY

MUST MAKE THE KAIJU
    PAY FOR WHAT IT DID

NEVER LET YOUR CREW DOWN

SHOOT FIRST AND LET
    SOMEONE ELSE FILL
    OUT THE PAPERWORK

Lab Mode Aspects

There are a lot of strange elements in a world full of giant monsters and robots. This aspect highlights how you handle the strange technology, the constant worry of kaiju attack, and how to turn disaster into profit. How do you feel about kaiju? How do you feel about the corporations? This aspect reflects what you do when someone comes to you with a strange bit of technology or piece of a kaiju to inspect.

Lab Mode Aspects

STILL BELIEVES IN Z-WAVES
KAIJU GOURMET
INFECTED BY K-TEK GREMLINS
NO PROBLEM A K-TEK
   GADGET CAN'T HANDLE
ALWAYS "IMPROVING" DESIGNS

OTAKAIJU TRIVIA MASTER
SECRET FREEZILLY
RESEARCH IS FOR THE WEAK
MULTIPLE DOCTORATES
THE TRUTH IS OUT THERE

Office Mode Aspects

This mode reflects how you're seen around the offices of the company you work for. Some people do well in the mundane office environment, others like to work alone. This aspect also reflects how important the job is to your character. Is it just a paycheck? Is it a life's passion? Is it a stepping stone to something greater? A good Office mode aspect not only reflects where your character is right now but where they see themselves in five years.

Office Mode Aspects

ALWAYS REMEMBERS
   IMPORTANT INFO
   (LIKE BIRTHDAYS)
UNOFFICIAL IT GEEK
THE MASTER OF GOSSIP
I JUST WORK HERE
LOOKING BUSY IS BETTER
   THAN BEING BUSY

A TERMINAL CASE OF
   THE MONDAYS
FRESH-FACED COLLEGE
   GRADUATE
MY DAD GOT ME THIS JOB
SLEEPING MY WAY TO
   THE MIDDLE
ASSISTANT (TO THE)
   REGIONAL MANAGER

PR Mode Aspects

This mode reflects how you interact with other people outside the office. It can be about your professional reputation, your personal attitude, or how people perceive you as a part of the kaiju industry. Do you make the kaiju corporations look good? Do you come across as sincere? Do people trust you immediately or must you work at it? These aspects often reflect how working for a big company can change a person without them knowing it.

PR Mode Aspect

FREEZILLY SELLOUT

LIKE A GAME SHOW HOST

NO COMMENT

A SMILE LIKE YOUR MOM'S

NEVER LET THEM SEE YOU SWEAT

DO I HAVE TO GO TO THE PRESS CONFERENCE?

DRESSED TO THE NINES

NO TIE WITHOUT A KETCHUP STAIN

MULTI-MILLION DOLLAR ENDORSEMENT DEAL

DOESN'T BELIEVE IN STRAIGHT ANSWERS

Interview Aspect

Your fifth and final character aspect is created at the table after you've completed the rest of your character sheet (page 96). Leave it blank for now. If you're still stumped after your interview, we've got some basic suggestions below.

Interview Aspects

I DON'T CARE WHAT YOU THINK

IMPRESSIVE WORK HISTORY

COMPLETELY UNQUALIFIED FOR THE JOB

STRANGE HOBBIES

DROPPED THE LAWSUIT TO GET REHIRED

MUSICIAN IN MY SPARE TIME

MY PERSONAL LIFE IS IN SHAMBLES

THIRD GENERATION EMPLOYEE

INDUSTRIAL SPY

UNDERCOVER REPORTER

HYBRID ABILITIES

For decades, the kaiju corporations denied that their consumer products had dangerous side effects. That's still the official line with Legal, but one of the unspoken truths of a kaiju consumer society is that the corporations downplay or ignore any side effects. The corporations have started to really push the envelope with this idea by splicing employees with kaiju DNA. Some companies have done so with willing test subjects. Conspiracy theories suggest that long-term exposure to kaiju projects may also have side effects and that these studies are being hidden by the kaiju corporations.

If your character has one of these abilities, they are a little more than human but far less than kaiju. Chances are, the company that did this to the character will want to keep a close eye on their investment. If the character was altered willingly, they are now a corporate asset with a higher value. If they were altered unwillingly, the corporation might take action to make sure the character doesn't find out the truth. Better make sure those time sheets are filled out properly.

Hybrid Aspects

Access to hybrid stunts (page 26) requires a **hybrid aspect** that connects the character to the setting either through one of the monsters or one of the corporations. If the aspect connects to a monster, that monster will feature in a lot of crisis moments. If the aspect connects to a company, the plots discussed in the setting history will come to light at the table.

Hybrid aspects

MY MOTHER'S BUG EYES

HOVERS OFF THE GROUND WHEN EXCITED

BABAYAGITCH DOUBLE AGENT

THIRD-GENERATION KANEDA

SPEAKS FLUENT BLOBSTERA

HEIGHTENED THORZILLA BIOELECTRIC FIELD

DISGRUNTLED Z-WAVE HOLDOUT

WEBBED FINGERS HIDDEN IN MITTENS

HAWKESBURY SAVED MY PARENTS

ESCAPED FROM A GWAI FACILITY LAST YEAR

STEP FIVE: CHOOSE YOUR STUNTS

Each character starts with three stunts and three refresh. Stunts are grouped by modes and each mode chosen for the character should have at least one stunt. Additional stunts can be purchased for one refresh each, though hybrid stunts may only be selected or purchased by characters that selected hybrid aspects (page 24). We've included a list broken down by each stunt. Take the ones here to get a quick start, use them for inspiration, or create brand-new ones using the guidelines in *Fate Core*.

Crisis Mode Stunts

Come Get Some: Gain a +2 to Combat attack actions while dealing with a danger aspect.

Compromised Cameras: When creating an advantage using Tradecraft, gain a free invoke on any aspect created involving security cameras.

Rock Climbing Enthusiast: Gain a +2 to Fitness overcome actions when climbing.

Lab Mode Stunts

And I Even Like the Color: Once per game, you may cancel stress equal to your Operate roll during a conflict while operating a vehicle. Once the conflict is over, the vehicle is totaled.

Hacker Extraordinaire: Gain a +2 to Technology overcome actions when accessing a hostile system.

Weapons Designer: Roll Technology instead of Combat when attacking with a K-Tek weapon of your own design.

Office Mode Stunts

Bullied in School: Gain a +2 to Ambition defend actions when someone uses Provoke to insult or taunt you.

Digging In the Dirt: If you succeed with style on a Networking roll, create a BLACKMAIL aspect with two free invokes.

I Always Bring Cupcakes: Gain a +2 to Rapport create advantage actions when getting a named character from your office to help you out.

PR Mode Stunts

Get Them Out of My Sight: When you succeed with style on a Provoke attack roll, gain a LINGERING RESENTMENT aspect with one free invoke.

Good Cop: Gain a +2 to Empathy overcome actions when trying to get someone to talk about something they don't want to say.

We're With the Band: Once per game, you can get a number of people up to your Spin rating inside a secure facility by bluffing your way through the front door.

Hybrid Stunts

Hybrid stunts are slightly more powerful than normal stunts. Whenever a character uses a hybrid stunt, the GM gets a fate point for their **fate budget** (page 52), which they can use to invoke an NPC's aspects. Additionally, if a GM has a hybrid NPC and their stunt affects a player character, that player is awarded a fate point. If more than one player is affected, the player with the fewest fate points gets the award. In the case of a tie, the GM chooses. The player always chooses if a hybrid stunt is activated by their character.

Regeneration: Reduce a consequence related to physical injury by one level. You may not remove a mild consequence.

Hypnotic Pupils: When you succeed on a Rapport roll, you may choose to succeed with style.

Creepy Wings: Create an IN THE AIR aspect with a free invoke.

Gecko Feet: Succeed at a Fitness skill roll when overcoming an obstacle through climbing.

Raptor Claws: Give a consequence inflicted by a hand-to-hand Combat roll an additional free invoke.

STEP SIX: THE FINAL INTERVIEW

To finish up your crew, the GM gathers everyone's character sheet into a single pile and shuffles them face-down. You'll be doing a short scene to get everyone a little bit into character. This scene reflects a few moments from the character's final interview with Human Resources before they got the job on your kaiju crew.

Flip over the top sheet on the stack and review it with the group. When you pass it back to the player, you may begin the scene in the interview room, with you and the other players taking on the role of the interview panel. The GM should take the lead in setting up the interview scene and ask the first question if possible. Ask the player about elements of their character, hypothetical job situations, previous job experience, or even trot out those standard job interview questions that always get asked that nobody likes.

Wrap up the scene after the interviewee has answered one to three questions. They will then decide what aspect might come out from their answers. If the player is having trouble deciding on an aspect, open up discussion with the rest of the table. Once the player has chosen their aspect, select the next character sheet at random and repeat the process until all players have had their time in the hot seat. Everyone's character sheets will now have five complete aspects.

Rules Option: Direct Hire

The interview phase and the aspect that comes from it is inspired by Jared Sorensen's **Inspectres**. If you're looking for a game that mixes working stiffs dealing with the supernatural while lampooning some of reality TV's worst cliches, it's definitely worth checking out.

If your players don't have the time or the inclination to relive their last job interview, look to page 23 for inspiration, or replace this aspect with one reflecting the character's life away from the office. We've included a list of ones to inspire below.

Off-Duty Aspects

COLLECTS SPORES, MOLDS, AND FUNGUS	PARENTS DISAPPOINTED IN ME
KAIJU COSPLAYER	WHO DOESN'T LOVE CARS?
MOTHER OF FOUR	CHARITABLE CONTRIBUTIONS
WAS I FLIRTING?	TRYING TO START MY OWN BUSINESS
MOONLIGHTING AS A CAB DRIVER	BINGE WATCH WHENEVER I CAN

Example: Dr. Caleb Laramie

Kat gets together with Mesa, Louise, and their GM Lamar to make characters. While discussing ideas, they play a round or two of the card game **Kaiju Incorporated** to get into the setting. They decide to be a corporate crew, with Kat as the crew's scientist. She wants to play against the nerdy lab-rat type and have her character be more in the mold of Indiana Jones or Ian Malcolm. Caleb Laramie pops into her head as a name, which she writes at the top of her character sheet.

Looking at the modes, she wants Lab mode at Good (+3), to represent her character's knowledge of technology and Kaiju. Crisis mode is next at Fair (+2), since she wants to be able to handle any scrapes in the field. PR mode is her last selection at Average (+1), to represent a bit of charisma. By not choosing Office mode, we know that office politics are not a strong suit with Laramie.

Kaiju Studies becomes Laramie's focus in Lab mode. In Crisis mode, Fitness seems like the best pick for someone running and jumping a lot. Kat chooses Spin as her character's PR focus for a bit of roguish charm. Kat really wants to be able to rattle off kaiju facts and determine weak points of a monster, so she chooses to specialize in Kaiju Studies. She adds "Dr." in front of Caleb Laramie's name at the top of the character sheet. Dr. Laramie starts with three stress boxes since Fitness is trained but Ambition is not.

The first couple of Dr. Laramie's aspects come quickly. RENEGADE KAIJU BIOLOGIST ends up as his high concept and THAT'S DOCTOR TO YOU, PAL fits his Lab mode. ROGUISH CHARM sums up Laramie's PR mode after Kat deliberates on it for a few minutes. She doesn't want Laramie to be a fighter but she also doesn't see him as a coward. She smiles and writes down his fourth aspect—COOL UNDER PRESSURE. That will help him out in a crisis but might also compel him when other people ask him to do dangerous things.

Kat considers whether or not she wants hybrid stunts for Dr. Laramie. Being tied to a corporation doesn't sound like something he'd do, so she opts for regular stunts. She creates **I've Been Going Over The Data**, which gives her a +2 to create advantage using Kaiju Studies on kaiju Dr. Laramie has encountered before. She wants Laramie to be able to break and enter reliably, so she gives him a **Kaiju Bone Lockpick Set**. Finally, Dr. Laramie has **Old Flames Everywhere**, which allows Kat to declare an NPC as one of Caleb's old lovers once per game.

Once everyone else has finished up their characters, the group settles in for the interview phase. The other players ask about where Dr. Laramie got his degree and what his first field experience was. Based on the scene, Kat gets the feeling Laramie isn't exactly respected by other scientists, so she chooses SHADY ACADEMIC REPUTATION as her interview aspect.

Dr. Caleb Laramie

ASPECTS

High Concept:
RENEGADE KAIJU BIOLOGIST
Aspects: THAT'S DOCTOR TO YOU, PAL; ROGUISH CHARM;
COOL UNDER PRESSURE
Interview Aspect: SHADY ACADEMIC REPUTATION

MODES & SKILLS

Good (+3) LAB	Fair (+2) CRISIS	Average (+1) PR
Kaiju Studies**:	**Fitness***:	**Spin***:
Superb (+5)	Good (+3)	Fair (+2)
Operate:	**Combat:**	**Empathy:**
Good (+3)	Fair (+2)	Average (+1)
Technology:	**Tradecraft:**	**Provoke:**
Good (+3)	Fair (+2)	Average (+1)

STUNTS

I've Been Going Over The Data:
Gain +2 to create advantage using Kaiju Studies on kaiju Dr. Laramie has encountered before.

Kaiju Bone Lockpick Set: Gain +2 on Tradecraft rolls to overcome mechanical locks.

Old Flames Everywhere: Once per game, you may declare that you've had a romantic entanglement with an NPC. Create an IT'S COMPLICATED advantage with one free invoke.

STRESS ☐☐☐

CONSEQUENCES

Mild (2)
Moderate (4)
Severe (6)

THE KAIJU AND THE CORPORATIONS

A HISTORY OF DESTRUCTION AND REBIRTH

The world as we know it was changed by the appearance of kaiju. It's hard to imagine what things would be like without the likes of Queen Ghirodellora or Thorzilla shaking things up every few years. What would the Tokyo skyline be without the neon purple logo of Kaijumoto Keiretsu lighting up the night? What would people do with their smartphones if they couldn't check Monstergram photos of their friends? What would Dai-Burger serve as its Gutbuster Challenge? To understand the world today, one must go back to the moment when things changed.

1950S: DAIKAIJU RAVAGES TOKYO

The origins of the giant monsters now commonly called kaiju are still debated today. Some believe they are ancient creatures awoken from the sea by our nuclear testing. Others think they are mutations brought on by alien meteorites interacting with inhabitants of the planet. All, some, or none of these theories could be correct. What scientists can agree on is that kaiju have changed the planet completely in the past few decades and few humans haven't felt their influences either by surviving a kaiju attack or owning a product made possible by the research on these strange beasts.

The mystery of the kaiju began in October 1954, when local fishermen began to go missing off the coast of Japan. Authorities chalked it up to choppy seas and bad weather, but when a warship was discovered with all aboard electrocuted and a nearby freighter seemingly torn in two, those in power took it seriously. Japanese officials dispatched Dr. Hideo Kaneda to investigate and he returned with a terrible discovery. A giant creature was the cause of the attacks and it was only a matter of time before it ravaged a populated area. He called it Daikaiju, after the term for "big strange beast" the local fishermen had given the monstrosity.

Daikaiju defied science as we knew it by its very existence. It was sixty meters tall with a reptile body and two eel-like tentacles for arms. The arms generated massive bioelectricity that swept aside tanks and military vehicles like dust bunnies. It bellowed in a voice that shattered windows blocks away from the destruction.

A meter-long tooth, discovered in the first ravaged freighter, draws tourists to the main lobby of Kaijumoto Keiretsu in Osaka. Though other kaiju have since been bigger or possessed more terrifying abilities, none had more global impact than Daikaiju did when it revealed itself to the world.

On November 6th, 1954, the creature stepped out of the tall tales of fishermen and hypotheses of fringe scientists into downtown Tokyo. The nuclear devastation seen by the world at the end of World War II paled in comparison to what Daikaiju brought to Japan. The arrival of NATO and Soviet Bloc forces on November 11th heralded the beginning of Operation: Blanket Pedal. The armies aggressively attacked and pursued Daikaiju and threw millions of dollars in equipment, manpower, and ammunition at the beast.

Only the combined efforts of nearly a dozen world militaries stopped Daikaiju from destroying Honshu and rendering Japan no more. For those few days, the world came together to unite against a larger threat. Even with such powerful military backing, the armed forces only succeeded in driving Daikaiju back into the sea. There were many who hoped that by showing the human race was no longer at the top of the planet's food chain, everyone would come together to address all the strife, politics, and selfish desires that pushed the world to the brink of destruction.

Unfortunately, humanity's base nature intervened. Each nation that went up against Daikaiju looked towards weaponization or exploitation instead of education or prevention. Skirmishes broke out over scales, fluids, and other pieces Daikaiju left behind. Scientists considered experts in the field were kidnapped or convinced to defect to other countries. One more race to discovery added to the tensions between the East and the West. The winner of the atom race would find a power source that would push humanity to the future. The winner of the space race would lead humanity to the stars. The winner of the kaiju race would protect the world.

As part of Japan's reconstruction, the nations of the world funneled millions of dollars to a defense project lead by Dr. Kaneda. Kaneda traveled the globe seeking top scientists, veterans of the battle with Daikaiju, and other experts who believed the attack on Tokyo was only the first of many. This loose group of academics, soldiers, and fortune hunters were proven right when other attacks occurred within a year of the Tokyo disaster. Many of these creatures were caught and shipped to a top-secret island where they could be studied and monitored. The governments of the world knew about Menagerie Island, but the public was unaware—for the moment.

1960S: KAIJU AROUND THE WORLD

Despite the regular stream of kaiju attacks in the Pacific Ocean, most governments did little to protect their people. The US and Soviet Union were happy to sell weapons to countries affected and concentrated on outdoing each other in nearly every other area of production and propaganda. At best, a few proxy battles between weapons built to battle kaiju were fought in Southeast Asia. Most of America's focus on kaiju was how to use terror and paranoia to get an advantage on its enemies.

That all changed on September 19th, 1965. The first kaiju attack on American soil devastated San Francisco. The kaiju Kudzus tore apart the Golden Gate Bridge as if it were made of tissue paper. The fire that finally defeated the green menace also ravaged the city, leaving many to wonder if the means to destroy the beast were worth the price paid. It left terrible fungus spores in its wake that still plague the city to this day, since a new Kudzus could grow from these remains. Only a lucky southeasterly wind and the Mojave Desert have prevented a widespead dispersion of the kaiju.

The Soviets had little time to relish the suffering of their enemy. A few months later, the kaiju Thorzilla tore through the Baltic Sea and cut a path of destruction through Latvia, Estonia, and several countries under the protection of the Soviet Union. Moscow had made the terrible mistake of concentrating its kaiju defenses on the Eastern coastline. Nobody had expected kaiju to come from anywhere besides the Pacific Ocean. By the time the Soviet Union mobilized its defenses to capture Thorzilla, many Eastern European cities had already been reduced to electrically charged, smoking rubble. The kaiju Thorzilla and Kudzus had just lashed out at both of the world's nuclear superpowers and stunned both giants with their destruction.

Meanwhile, on Menagerie Island, Dr. Kaneda's research hit upon a fruitful vein. Rather than detonating nuclear weapons to destroy kaiju, he suggested using that energy to power a machine that could stand up to the monsters and fight like them. These *batteboto* machines would use highly-trained pilots to react to creatures in ways jet fighters and tanks could not. The first kaiju Ace, Dino Solomon, launched the first *batteboto* from Menagerie Island to fend off an attack by Anginus. The picture of Solomon standing on the shoulder of *Lotus Vow*, who in turn stood atop Anginus's motionless body, became one of the most unforgettable images of the decade.

The construction of *Lotus Vow* opened up a new field in the competition between the US and Russia. The defeat of Anginus proved the feasibility of *batteboto* as defense technology. Both countries snapped up as many members of Kaneda's team as they could to put them to work on their own designs. Menagerie Island also went into business refining their *batteboto*. The intelligence community spent much of their time stealing, destroying, and reverse engineering designs. The famous Ian St. James spy films were born out of this intrigue, spawning such hits as *Dr. Kan*, *You Only Roar Twice*, and *Kaiju Are Forever*.

The tension between the two nations came to a head in a two-week period in October of 1967. The recently developed Tomoyuki-Cooper Kaiju Alert system indicated an imminent kaiju attack on a small island located between Florida and Cuba. Cuba asked for the Soviet Union to send a *batteboto* to protect Havana from the kaiju called El Niño. Moscow obliged by sending *Winter Stalemate* to stand guard. The US sent its own *boto*, *Thunder Flash*, and stationed it in Miami. While the kaiju Aces waited, they traded insults and boasts, which left many wondering if the Aces would escalate to an actual brawl and drag both armies into World War III. When El Niño never showed up, the *batteboto* were ordered to stand down. Ask any historian and they'll say the Cuban Kaiju Crisis was the closest the world has come to utterly destroying itself.

1970S: THE RISE OF
THE KAIJU INDUSTRY

The world took a darker turn in the 1970s. Nations were mired in wars, conflicts, and other sticky situations. The economy took a turn for the worse. The optimism of the previous decade leaked out of the world like air from a balloon. Kaiju attacks were the norm rather than the exotic, if dangerous, distraction they had been. Kaiju Aces settled into the same level of celebrity as rock stars and professional athletes and busied themselves with petty rivalries and product endorsements. With so many posturing Aces waiting for disaster to strike, their novelty wore thin.

The arms race between the West and the East built several *batteboto* but rarely ended up using them. The two industrial powers outpaced each other with dozens of robots and not enough kaiju to fight them all. In the rush to get the most robots in the field, countries broke barriers with kaiju Aces in rapid succession. Russia fielded the first female kaiju Ace. America responded with the first African American Ace. These may have been calculated moves born out of the Public Relations office but it leveled the playing field for anyone who wanted a shot at sitting in the cockpit and facing down a kaiju. But as new faces were hired, older Aces watched their robots be decommissioned without ever facing a kaiju in the field.

Even Menagerie Island wasn't immune to the financial troubles of the decade. Countries spent most of their budgets on building robots instead of researching new kaiju. The island's equipment was out of date and badly needed repair. Dr. Kaneda could barely keep kaiju from escaping on a regular basis. The island was unable to take in new kaiju that were defeated by kaiju Aces, but nobody else wanted to pay for their care and feeding. Dr. Kaneda spent more and more time in his lab, hoping to find a solution in science.

Moments like these cause good people to make bad decisions. Dino Solomon, famous pilot of the *Lotus Vow*, fell on hard times. Ten years had passed since he was sitting on top of the world. Two failed marriages and a drinking problem were all that held the pilot together when he visited his old friend Dr. Kaneda on Menagerie Island. Solomon had an idea to fix everyone's problems. Some of his connections in New York wanted to acquire a kaiju for an exhibition. Kaneda was reluctant, but when Solomon suggested that these connections might collect the thousands of dollars Dino owed in gambling debts in far more gruesome ways, the deal was struck. The captive kaiju Queen Conga was shipped to New York and arrived on December 17th, 1976. Dino Solomon was on top of the world for that week as the face of the Radio City Kaiju Revue. It wouldn't last.

Exactly what angered Queen Conga is still unclear. Photography flashes, the lights of Manhattan, or the energy of New York City agitated her. New York had avoided a major clash with a kaiju up to that point. On Christmas Eve, Queen Conga roared through Manhattan like it was her own private island. She leapt from building to building, leaving paw prints in the Empire State Building and World Trade Center. A lucky missile strike caught her in midair and brought her down to street level, where she was finally subdued.

Dino was hung out to dry by his criminal connections. The media quickly discovered his meeting with Dr. Kaneda and their funding arrangement. The ensuing scandal (dubbed "Conga Eve" by the media) cut Menagerie Island off from government funding. One by one, countries pulled out of their investments, and where the money went, personnel followed.

In the space of a year, Menagerie Island went from the leading think tank of kaiju experts to a shell of its former self. The United States and Soviet Union threatened to destroy the island with a nuclear strike, but both sides were afraid that such an act would trigger a larger exchange. The superpowers quietly hoped that the monsters on the island would battle themselves to death.

Dr. Kaneda knew that letting the kaiju collected on the island roam free would be a disaster that would make Daikaiju's destruction of Tokyo look like a child's temper tantrum. Kaneda called in every favor he had with private industries and convened a meeting at Houshi Hokuriku, the world's oldest hotel. His goal was to protect the world from a sudden onslaught of kaiju, but he knew the only way he could get the businesses on board was to convince them of the kaiju's profitability. He focused on short-term lucrative defense contracts while hinting at a future of kaiju-based consumer products.

No sooner had Kaijumoto Keiretsu come together under Dr. Kaneda than three other companies stepped in to try their hand at making money in the kaiju industry. Starr Industries moved to consolidate and buy out all the other kaiju defense manufacturers in the US. Australian shipping tycoon Montgomery Hawkesbury, already rich from developing ships and other vehicles that could safely transport kaiju to Menagerie Island, founded Hawkesbury Limited to start shipping monsters and salvage equipment to an abandoned tract of land in the Outback. Even the scandal-ridden Dino Solomon was able to pull together a band of investors to form Z-Wave, perhaps best known for their line of dubious kaiju detection electronics looking for "Z-energy particles" supposedly radiating from all kaiju. Most of these devices were Geiger counters or radio wave detectors decorated with little extra bits of flash. Dino's pitchman charisma, and the 2:00 a.m. airtime of their commercials, lured in enough customers for Z-Wave to stay in sight of their competitors and even start building *batteboto* to increase awareness for their brand.

1980S: ONLY BUY GENUINE KAIJU PRODUCTS

The birth of the kaiju corporations refreshed the stumbling *batteboto* industry. Each corporation wanted their own kaiju Aces front and center. These new Aces weren't waiting around for an alert; they were ambassadors for the companies that sponsored them. The old Aces were free to do as they pleased so long as they did their jobs when the time came to battle kaiju. Corporate Aces were expected to toe the line far more carefully and not end up in gossip magazines. This shift caused trouble for some Aces as the industry headed into a decade known for its decadence.

Montgomery Hawkesbury tested out new robots in his secret game reserve full of the refugees from Menagerie Island. Though he still made money transporting kaiju between the other corporations, Hawkesbury found the real key to increasing his prestige was offering the rich a chance to part with a percentage of their fortune to hunt kaiju on their own. These hunters didn't have the time to train as proper pilots, so Hawkesbury developed a smaller version of the *batteboto* suit he called a "robozoid." The industrial applications soon became apparent, but their original intent, like any robot suit armed to the gills with state-of-the-art weaponry, was to take down kaiju. Rather than one-on-one clashes towering over buildings, Hawkesbury developed a pack hunter method that tired the beast out.

A MATCH MADE IN MARYLAND

Z-Wave, desperate to be seen as a contemporary of the other kaiju corporations, launched its own military *batteboto* design. The latest in computer technology rendered the need for a kaiju Ace unnecessary, and Z-Wave's proprietary computational intelligence system had a memory rating of 100 zetabytes. Mechaconga was activated to chase down another attack by Queen Conga on the Eastern Seaboard of the United States. The two met on the field of battle...and it was love at first sight. The kaiju hunter went rogue. The Match Made in Maryland left Z-Wave with egg on its face even if the torrid love affair did save Baltimore from kaiju destruction.

The executives at competitor Kaijumoto Keiretsu noticed something strange in the aftermath of The Match Made in Maryland. Focus groups responding to their latest batch of Ace cadets reported that they had favorite kaiju too. The company never imagined consumers would start to show sympathy for the monsters. Kaijumoto was ready to release a new line of *batteboto* electronic toys and made the controversial decision to delay the line so they could add kaiju toys for the robots to battle. The gamble paid off with short supplies of Kaiju Kommand making the news on a weekly basis. The media dubbed the frenzy "Kaiju Kristmas" and the trend of kaiju-based releases being spelled differently to be unique in the marketplace started soon after.

The success of the Kaiju Kristmas campaign stunned Starr Industries executives. For years, their sole exploitation of kaiju had been selling defense products to militaries. The public clearly had a hunger for kaiju consumer products and Starr was going to beat Kaijumoto to market with as many as possible. On August 23, 1985, Starr Industries rebranded as Monstersanto to roll out a wide variety of consumer products beyond the high-end toys of their Japanese competitor and the low-end junk of Z-Wave. If Kaijumoto made money making products based on kaiju, Monstersanto would give the public products made with kaiju.

1990S: EVERYBODY LOVES KAIJU

As the '80s wore on, the kaiju corporations' plans to turn kaiju into marketable assets worked all too too well. They wanted to generate a connection to the kaiju to encourage consumers to buy more products, but they also cultivated sympathy for the beasts. For the first time, people wanted kaiju to be treated like living beings, not just things to be hunted, killed, and studied. There was still a market for what the kaiju corporations made but a growing backlash meant they had to tread carefully when expanding their business.

Kaijumoto Keiretsu looked to take back the market that Monstersanto claimed after Kaiju Kristmas. It deployed a fascinating piece of K-Tek on a kaiju discovered in Antarctica. The kaiju was controlled by a helmet that allowed direct mental communication. Most kaiju make their presence known with a sudden attack that devastates a city. Gatchamanera arrived during a major Thanksgiving Day parade in New York, waving to the people below and touring the world that year for pictures and other press opportunities. Kaiju were now in the limelight as much as kaiju Aces.

Thanks to the marketing blitz of the previous decade and the success of Gatchamanera's launch, a new type of kauji superfan arrived. The *otakaiju* were made up of the boys and girls that grew up with '80s kaiju cartoons and cereal but now had more disposable income. They wanted deluxe figures, photo-accurate kaiju Ace costumes, and authentic pieces of kaiju preserved in airtight containers. These fans soon became a headache for kaiju crews trying to keep civilians safe. Most people have the common sense to run away from a giant rampaging monster. *Otakaiju* run towards the monster so they can get some great pictures and maybe a scoop of slime to sell on the internet.

All the *otakaiju* needed to do to get a taste of kaiju was walk down to their local burger joint. Fast-food restaurants had been offering kaiju toys and endorsements from kaiju Aces for years. Monstersanto took the next step by opening the first Dai-Burger in Appleton, Wisconsin, on September 19th, 1992. Most of the food was typical fare, but the CongaBurger was made with a secret percentage of kaiju meat. Countless theories abounded as to where the meat came from, ranging from a deep freeze locker located in Antarctica to a clone program somewhere in New Jersey.

Patrons couldn't decide on what it tasted like—some said chicken, some said beef, some said fish. The mystery bolstered demand and franchises spread like a virus through the world. On May 20th, 1998, Dai-Burger opened its 1000th restaurant in Times Square, New York City. The entrance was specially customized to look like patrons were walking into the mouth of Daikaiju.

Support for the ethical treatment of kaiju grew in the early '90s. When word leaked that Z-Wave was experimenting on cloned Thorzilla tissue, Z-Wave offices soon found themselves swamped in protests. They adopted the derisive name "Freezillys" given to them by corporate media, and pushed back against kaiju exploitation. Most kaiju rights activists were content with staging sit-ins, circulating petitions on college quads, and occasionally scrawling "Die Burger!" across the front of a fast-food restaurant in red paint. With public opinion on their side, it would take a serious incident to get the corporations out of the hot seat.

On June 9th, 1993. Montgomery Hawkesbury was on the cusp of living his life-long dream. Flush from the success of releasing unarmed robozoids as luxury vehicles to the civilian market, he unveiled his next ambitious project. His company had fought and captured many kaiju, all for a singular purpose—to open a preserve where people could safely see kaiju in their natural majesty. Land of the Lost Valley was set to open on La Isla del Toro, a few hundred miles away from several Mexican resorts.

Hackers claiming to work for the Freezilly movement caused a massive systems failure that let the kaiju loose on the island. Of the dozens of staff members on site to prepare for the park's opening, only five survived. Hawkesbury sacrificed himself to give those five enough time to escape on his personal helicopter by luring the kaiju in the opposite direction of the helipad.

Z-Wave's second attempt at a *batteboto* revolution only required half of a giant robot. Their Thorzilla tissue research resulted in Mechathor, another attempt to fight kaiju without kaiju Aces. Information leaked by Freezillys forced the company to release Mechathor early. The creature went wild, seeking out its parent in a clash between kaiju that wrecked Reykjavik. The Freezillys countered with photocopied documents showing that Z-Wave knew the Mechathor project was a disaster.

Kaiji corporation legal teams used the death of Montomgery Hawkesbury and the Mechathor disaster to go after the Freezilly community hard. Nearly overnight, public opinion turned against the Freezillys. Kaiju corporations joined together to crush their opposition by keeping up the public pressure and pushing for laws with harsh penalties for interfering in corporate business. The companies used the Lost Valley incident to tilt as much as they could in their favor, such as lowering safety standards in factories, busting unions, and making kaiju material claims easy for them but difficult for consumers. These new laws let the corporations dive into areas they had previously feared for ethical and legal concerns. The Big Four were on the top of the world. The only direction left to go was down.

2000S: TURBULENCE AT THE TOP

The turn of the century came with a bang, not a whimper. The bill came due for years of building and buying on credit, and nobody wanted to pay up. The decade was filled with sped-up cycles of boom and bust as new ideas pulled companies out of obscurity and cast down institutions. Corporations sank the cutting edge of science into kaiju research to push K-Tek farther out than anyone could have ever imagined. By the end of the decade, each of the major corporations would be changed in irrevocable ways, and a new company would rise out of the ashes of another.

Z-Wave never completely recovered from the Mechaconga and Mechathor fiascos. During the economic turbulence of the early part of the decade, Z-Wave's stock dropped to an all-time low. Most employees wrote off these sorts of stock fluctuations as part of working for Z-Wave. When the doors of the company's offices in Los Angeles were found locked one morning, something had changed. Creditors had gotten tired of waiting for Z-Wave to climb out of the hole. The other major corporations, eager to pick over the company's bones for the most useful bits, released every bit of dirt and rumor they had. The loss of a kaiju corporation shook investor confidence. Not only had the company forced hundreds of people out of work, it dragged the stock market down with it. Crash Wednesday gave notice to everyone that even the kaiju corporations weren't immune to the laws of economics.

Sensing a change in the wind, Dr. Hideo Kaneda announced his retirement shortly after the dissolution of Z-Wave. The pioneer of the study of kaiju and the inventor of the K-Tek concepts had doubts about his legacy. He knew that staying connected with the company he created would interfere with the serious scientific study of the kaiju. Even with this noble intent, Dr. Kaneda was not above human error. He named his son Artemis Kaneda as his replacement within Kaijumoto. Hideo walked a line between respecting the kaiju and knowing how to use them to keep his projects funded. Artemis, growing up as the spoiled scion of a burgeoning industry, just wanted to see profits rise.

Even after the disaster at the Land of the Lost Valley, Hawkesbury's surviving Board of Directors had an impressive inventory of captured kaiju. The company approached zoos across the world looking to lease their remaining kaiju as attractions. Most zoos declined the opportunity over fears the beasts would get loose and the zoo would go down in history like Conga Eve or the Lost Valley incident. Hawkesbury introduced new safety protocols, including only leasing a single kaiju per zoo and having an ex-kaiju Ace on hand as a safety advisor. The organizations that took Hawkesbury up on their offer soon found themselves rolling in cash. Kaiju finally broke into smaller markets thanks to the KaijuZoo program.

Monstersanto looked to repeat the success of Dai-Burger by expanding into other types of cuisine at their restaurants. They were also trying to get in front of competitors who were attempting to break off market shares from the burger giant. Giant pizzas from Pete Zilla, a two-pound burrito from Taco Gahzonga, and Atomic Breath Wings from Ace's Pub all debuted within months of each other. Kaiju meat soon rose to a premium price and Monstersanto squeezed supplies to force competition out of the market. Some of its rivals struggled so much that when Monstersanto offered a buy-out, they sold gladly. Out of the kaiju cuisine franchise that rose up during this period, only Mama's Osaka Fried Kaiju remains independent of the food giant.

Kaijumoto, Hawkesbury, and Monstersanto picked apart Z-Wave when it folded, taking the best and brightest parts of the corporation. The rest of Z-Wave's assets were quietly acquired by one of two companies. Babayagitch debuted toward the end of the decade, rolling out the first major competitor to Kaijumoto's K-Phone with the slimmer, sleeker Roar-8. The company used an interesting tactic by marketing to the kaiju marketplace without using any sort of K-Tek or actual kaiju parts in the process of making the phone, such as a kaijuskin cover or Thorzilla conductors. No kaiju parts dropped the cost of the phone considerably, and Babayagitch soon made a name as the company providing consumers with kaiju-styled products without kaiju-sized prices. Babayagitch replaced Z-Wave as the fourth in the Big Four.

2010S: THE FASHIONABLE KAIJU OF TODAY

The other company that built itself out of Z-Wave's remains arrived without the usual fanfare of the kaiju industry. GWAI group quietly reverse engineered K-Tek devices made popular by other corporations and started selling cheaper versions. They have been careful enough to change designs just enough to avoid major lawsuits. GWAI's best products are the ones changed the least, such as their JPhone and their GhostBurgers franchise. The other competitors have sued anyway, leaving GWAI to ponder how to balance making money from its knockoffs while fending off legal challenges.

The other major legal battle still going on today is over robo-zoids. When the market plateaued in the late '90s, Hawkesbury introduced weapon mods that attached directly to the robozoids for the general public. Armed robozoids have been used by police and law enforcement for years, but passing those weapons directly to the general public has caused concern for safety. More recently, Hawkesbury quietly funded an alleged grassroots "open carry robozoid" movement to allow the project to continue. The internet is awash in KaiTube videos of users modifying their own robozoids to turn them into tiny *batteboto*.

Babayagitch leveraged its status as the kaiju company without kaiju to break into the actual kaiju market. Rather than natural kaiju, the company plans to push its synthetic kaiju to the next level. The company pioneers modified kaiju grown in a lab rather than capturing and harvesting kaiju. So far they've primarily grown kaiju parts for manufacturing purposes, but signs point to the company pushing for the first vat-grown, company-loyal kaiju to debut when Babayagitch announces the JPhone 10.

Monstersanto suffered a recent setback in its dominance of the kaiju foods segment. The Saladaze chain of healthy salad restaurants suffered a severe setback when it was revealed the Kudzus leaves used in the salads were linked to a strange disease where the victims gained a green tint to their skin, red coloration to their eyes, and an aggressive demeanor. Saladaze was poised to break out of its West Coast origins before the news hit, but now plans to expand the brand have come to a halt. Monstersanto hushed up many of these reports of tainted meals and chalked up the ones that got through to Freezilly bias in the media. Some claim that the managers of Saladaze restaurants were paid generously for their silence, but these rumors continue to go unfounded.

Dr. Kaneda passed away in his sleep at the beginning of 2015. With him died a simpler era before kaiju were on everyone's mind, plastered on buses, and sitting low in people's stomachs. News stories claim that Hideo and Artemis reconciled before the doctor died. Artemis, free of his responsibilities at Kaijumoto, assumed the duties of head of the Kaneda Institute and looks to work with the kaiju corporations as a partner in his endeavors. The more things change, the more they stay the same.

///KAIJU ATTACK///
THORZILLA
CANADA
CATEGORY 5
/CRISIS MODE/

///KAIJU ATTACK///
BLOBSTERA
COLOMBIA
CATEGORY 5
Countermeasures
Deployed

THE TOMOYUKI-COOPER
KAIJU ALERT SYSTEM
//00909299//

THE TOMOYUKI-COOPER KAIJU ALERT SYSTEM

Not every kaiju attack is created equal. Companies don't have the time and, more importantly, the money to send out a crew to every smashed barn or pool of radioactive goop discovered in a field somewhere. Kaiju crews need to be fresh and ready for when the real emergencies hit. Asset prioritization comes through a color-coded alert system that's the same across nations, companies, and the world. When a kaiju crew gets a message from the Tomoyuki-Cooper Kaiju Alert system, they know they are on the clock. A crew is usually dispatched to every type of alert, while the Aces wait for the big fights. An old kaiju crew saying goes, "Aces don't roll out of bed unless it's orange or red."

The TCKA bears the names of its creators, Ichiro Tomoyuki and Wallace Cooper. These scientists came together in the late '60s to study the frequency and ferocity of the rising kaiju attacks, classifying them using a color-coded system. They insisted it be adopted as the standard for every country fielding anti-kaiju technology,

to allow for better communication and coordination between military units. The United Nations Kaiju Agency still operates the TCKA system to this day.

Alerts apply to specific locations. They are coded to the specific attack rather than the strength of the kaiju. Sometimes a beast attacks when conditions are in its favor and it threatens an area especially susceptible to whatever strange powers it has at hand. Sometimes an attack hits an area full of substances the beast finds damaging and can't strike at full power. False calls are punishable by fines and jail time but every now and then someone gets a bright idea to fake a kaiju call to get their faces on the news or for some other petty motivation.

The first team on the scene of an alert lays claim to any kaiju resources left behind. This rule often comes under dispute in areas where a kaiju corporation has influence. A GWAI Group kaiju crew is not going to be welcomed to a TCKA call in Japan, nor would a Kaijumoto crew be able to freely access an alert near the Great Wall of China. The higher up the alert scale, the more flexible these scrabbles over turf become because of the emergency involved, but when the stakes are low, sometimes crews squabble, scrap, and sabotage to make sure they get the glory.

Blue Alert: No kaiju are currently in play at this alert level. Most of the world is technically in blue alert at all times, so this has come to mark areas where kaiju fighting forces stand idle or are rebuilding and repairing after a kaiju attack. At a Blue Alert, crews are on-call. This status evolved into slang for crews who say they've "got the blues" on days when they're working but not seeing any action. Most companies have their crews working four days on-call, then three days off during this alert level.

Green Alert: This level of alert means that kaiju activity is suspected but unconfirmed. This is often a smashed building or other evidence of a kaiju passing through the area. Biological evidence such as blood, mucus, or waste products are often reclassified as Yellow Alerts as soon as a crew arrives on the scene. Green Alerts feature the most interaction with the general public as the crew needs to interview witnesses and ask for help from local authorities during their investigation. Many members of a crew prefer a Green Alert status. The pay is better and they aren't stuck waiting around the office.

Yellow Alert: The danger of being in a kaiju crew increases significantly during a Yellow Alert. Yellow Alerts trigger when kaiju activity is confirmed but the monster is not currently being monitored. This usually happens before a monster attacks or if the monster's been repelled by a *batteboto* but the kill is not confirmed. Yellow Alerts are full of tension, since the kaiju is out there, somewhere, tearing a path of destruction. Crews responding to Yellow Alerts can sometimes be the first on the scene of an attack.

Orange Alert: This is the level where Aces get involved. Orange Alerts are active kaiju being monitored and may also be attacks on non-populated areas. Kaiju are often drawn to large industrial and population centers but they can decide to throw down anywhere, at any time, for any reason. Crews part of Orange Alerts are there to primarily assist Aces in keeping the attack from escalating further. They also take their normal roles of protecting civilians in danger from the fallout of any big battles between mecha and kaiju. Thrill-seeking crews only really consider themselves on the clock at this alert or higher.

Red Alert: This is the main event. Red Alerts are kaiju attacks on population centers, military facilities, and any other location where thousands of lives and millions of dollars are threatened. Aces are instructed to take down kaiju quickly and decisively during these battles. Often, multiple crews are on the scene to respond to situations caused by the mecha vs. kaiju battle. Red Alerts also mean coordinating with local emergency services who aren't trained to handle the unique problems that kaiju attacks bring to a big city.

Rumors exist, according to *otakaiju*, whistleblowers, and disgruntled ex-employees, of a secret alert level above Red. Code Black is believed to be an alert than can only be authorized by the head of state where the kaiju attack occurs, and allows for nuclear weapons to be used on their own soil. These rumormongers believe there was only one time in human history when Code Black was considered—if Operation Blanket Pedal had failed, the nuclear option would have been deployed. No creature since Daikaiju has brought the world as close to the brink, and these fringe fanatics claim that Daikaiju is still out there, waiting to finish the job.

SOUND THE ALARM! KAIJU ATTACK RULES

Now that you have a crew ready to stop disasters (and bill accordingly), it's time to throw some kaiju at them. We've included write-ups for every kaiju featured in the *Kaiju Incorporated* card game. You and your players will define the kaiju threat, and their crew will contend with the danger through challenges, contests, and conflicts. Don't worry if you're not feeling up to creating everything on the fly; we also have plenty of examples that you can use right out of the book.

KAIJU ATTACK CHECKLIST

Identify the Kaiju: Use a previously established kaiju or create one, spending nine points between **kaiju skills** Destruction, Terror, and Casualty.

Choose Alert Status: The Alert status determines how many **danger aspects** are on the board. Lower alerts are better suited for investigation while high alerts throw players into the middle of the action.

Choose Danger Aspects: Players choose skills to roll against the GM to see who creates the first danger aspect. Each side alternates until all aspects have been chosen.

Create Action Plans: Give the players some time to discuss how they want to tackle each of the danger aspects while you decide how best to frame these scenes as contests, conflicts, or challenges.

Laugh in the Face of Danger: Play out the scenes to determine whether or not the plans are successful. Successes with style during these scenes give players **gold stars** (page 56), which can help soothe the pain after unsuccessfully stopping a kaiju attack.

After Action Report: After the scenes are played out, determine whether the threat is eliminated, the threat continues, or the players punch out and accept consequences for their failure. If the players punch out, gold stars reduce the consequences individual players receive.

STEP ONE: IDENTIFY THE KAIJU

Kaiju have three **kaiju skills**: Destruction, Terror, and Casualty. The rating in the skill serves as the base difficulty for rolls the crews make when dealing with the problems caused by the kaiju. The GM can use them as a static difficulty or may roll if the situation fits. Crews rarely confront the kaiju directly, but they deal with complications and aftermath of kaiju attacks constantly.

Kaiju have nine points to split between these skills. For very quick creation, choose one at Great (+4), one at Good (+3), and one at Fair (+2). Or, draw a random kaiju card from the *Kaiju Incorporated* card game and use its corresponding entry from *Vogel's Kaiju Recognition Guide* on page 60. We've included examples of danger aspects related to each skill and how they play out in scenes.

Destruction

This represents the collateral damage caused by the kaiju. The crew has to deal with disasters to clear the area of civilians and rescue people trapped by the kaiju smashing through the area.

- ☢ Crumbling building
- ☢ Forest fire
- ☢ Flooded parking garage
- ☢ Collapsed stairway
- ☢ Stalled elevator

Example: Dr. Laramie needs to crawl down an elevator shaft to reach a pair of civilians trapped inside during an attack by Gahzonga. Gahzonga's Destruction is Great (+4) and Dr. Laramie's Fitness is Good (+3). Kat rolls a Superb (+5) result. Laramie rappels down the side of the shaft and gets the civilians to safety.

The Fate Pool and the Fate Budget

Fate Core has one general pool of fate points that collects from players when they invoke their aspects and awards players when they accept compels. Sometimes that makes the flow of fate points a little fuzzy when using aspects for GM characters.

The **fate budget** is a pool of points for the GM to use on NPCs that is kept separate from the general pool. Danger aspects created by the kaiju alert level also use the budget, since the situations these aspects reflect often create the antagonists that crews face. The fate budget starts at twice the number of players at the table and gains fate points when the GM accepts compels from character aspects and danger aspects. Fate points also go into the budget when players use their hybrid stunts.

Terror

This represents how panicked the general population gets when this kaiju shows up. Scared people do irrational things that the crew has to stop before they can get to work.

- ☢ Rioters
- ☢ Looters
- ☢ *Otakaiju* getting too close
- ☢ People fleeing from the kaiju towards a burning building (or vice versa)
- ☢ Overenthusiastic military leaders

> **Example:** No sooner has Dr. Laramie pulled the civilians up to the roof than a call comes in over his radio. The military is planning a bombing run to scare Gahzonga out of hiding and the building they're in is in the attack zone. Gahzonga's Terror is Fair (+2) and Laramie's Provoke is Average (+1). Kat rolls a -2 and decides to succeed at a cost because she's low on fate points. After a few moments of tense banter over the radio, the bomber captain agrees to abort the bomb run. Laramie sighs in relief, but one of his civilians, an eight year old boy, seems to have wandered off.

Casualty

This represents how dangerous the kaiju is to civilians. Aces focus on fighting the monster and expect the crew to handle any immediate threats to civilians in the combat zone.

- ☢ Damaged *batteboto* with an armed rocket payload
- ☢ Civilians caught in the crossfire
- ☢ Wounded first responders
- ☢ Amateur kaiju hunters
- ☢ Rookie kaiju Ace pushing a kaiju toward a hospital

> **Example:** The curious boy somehow crawled up on Gahzonga's sleeping form. Dr. Laramie needs to coax the boy across a ladder back to the safety of the rooftop. Gahzonga's Casualty is Good (+3) and Dr. Laramie's Rapport is Mediocre (+0). Kat's roll is a zero, but she invokes COOL UNDER PRESSURE and ROGUISH CHARM to get the kid off the beast. She decides to invoke RENEGADE KAIJU BIOLOGIST so she can succeed with style with a Fantastic (+6)! Dr. Laramie tosses his radio to the kid to plant on the sleeping beast and let the military pinpoint Gahzonga's location.

STEP TWO: CHOOSE ALERT STATUS

Situations arise during a kaiju attack that require the crew's intervention. These dangers can be disasters, civilians in the combat zone, or bureaucratic red tape that keeps the kaiju Ace from doing their job. It's up to the crew to put out these fires, literal and figurative, to keep people safe, and come home with some sweet stuff for the lab rats.

The severity of the TCKA determines how many danger aspects need to be created. Low alert status adventures often start out as mysteries that elevate into kaiju attacks. But if you want to open in the middle of a kaiju attack to get everybody's blood pumping, feel free to start off high.

TCKA Color	Danger Aspects
Blue	1
Green	2
Yellow	3
Orange	4
Red	5

STEP THREE: CREATE DANGER ASPECTS

After the number of aspects have been determined, it's time for everyone to assess the danger level of this particular encounter. Each of the players chooses one of their PC's skills that they think will come into play in the attack. They will likely pick one of their high skills. That's okay, since each player will be competing with the GM and the other players in the **assessment roll**.

The difficulty for the roll is the highest skill of the kaiju. Rolls that beat the difficulty give that player the chance to name a danger aspect. Any aspects left over are named by the GM. Rolls that tie in difficulty give the player a choice—they can name the danger aspect if it directly ties into their character, or the GM can declare the aspect.

Aspects are determined in alternating order. The players name an aspect, then the GM, until all aspects are complete.

STEP FOUR: CREATE ACTION PLANS

Give your crew some time to come up with a plan to deal with all the danger aspects. While they strategize, you should be thinking about which danger aspects are best suited to be addressed with a challenge, contest, or conflict.

Don't forget to compel players as they discuss their plans. Compels can determine who addresses what problems and even make things more difficult. The players can also compel those danger aspects right back to make sure the kaiju falls into their plans.

The crew might want to take on multiple problems at once. Splitting the party is okay, since it gives you scenes to bounce between. Good pacing can leave players excited as you cut from cliffhanger to cliffhanger and they try to solve two or more problems at the same time.

STEP FIVE:
LAUGH IN THE FACE OF DANGER

Each of the danger aspects generates either a conflict, contest, or challenge based on its nature. How successful the crew is in each activity determines how well they handle their role in the kaiju attack as a whole.

In addition to tracking the crew's successes and failures, also note whenever a player succeeds with style on a roll. In addition to the usual benefits of success with style, the character gets a **gold star**. Gold stars only matter during the **after action report** and only if the crew decides to break off from the current alert.

The Crisis Board

Before you dive in, set up your **crisis board.** There are a few ways to build your crisis board in the game. For maximum corporate synergy, we recommend using a dry erase whiteboard available at office supply stores everywhere. Veteran Fate players also likely have a good stash of index cards or sticky notes. Make a three-by-three grid and keep that on your side of the table. Aspects that are created in play should stay separate from the crisis board.

You can use Fate dice or Campaign Coins' Fate Tokens to keep track of progress on the crisis board. Set the die or token to ■ next to whichever aspects the players are currently dealing with. Then flip it over to a ✚ if the scene is successful, or a ▬ if the players failed. You can also mark gold stars when players succeed with style during each encounter.

Danger Challenges

- ☢ A building collapses with people inside. Roll against Destruction to get them to safety.
- ☢ You've got to reboot the *batteboto*'s weapon systems while it closes with the beast. Roll against Casualty to get the Ace completely back on line.
- ☢ Climb on the beast to use the tranquilizer device. Roll against Terror to stay firm and keep a good grip on the injector.

Danger Contests

- ☢ You have just the right device to stop the kaiju in your mobile unit. You need to roll K-Tek to find the darn thing once you get there. Roll against Destruction to get it before the city is trashed.
- ☢ You've got to clear a shopping mall that's directly in the creature's path. Roll against Terror to make sure everyone gets to safety.
- ☢ You've got to argue with the mayor to let you operate in his jurisdiction but his aide is trying to shut you down. Beat them in this contest to get the mayor to sign your paperwork.

Danger Conflicts

- ☢ A rival crew tries to jump your claim. They stay in the conflict until at least one of their own gets taken out.
- ☢ The kaiju Ace freezes up in the face of the monster's frightening power. You've got to rattle his cage to get him back in the fight. Provoke or empathize with him to get him to move.
- ☢ The kaiju has spawned something that's going after you. Take on a number of creatures equal to the kaiju's Casualty rating.

STEP SIX: AFTER ACTION REPORT

Once each danger aspect has been dealt with, count up the number of successes and failures on the crisis board. Each ⬛ moves the alert up a level, while ➕ moves it down. If you've moved the alert down past Blue, the attack is over and you've defeated the beast. If the alert moves up past Red, another crew has been called in to do what you could not. If the alert is still on the board, you can either stay on the job or punch out. If the crew punches out, each member suffers a consequence based on where the current alert status stands.

Consequences are reduced on individual characters by the number of gold stars they racked up during a scene (page 56). Only gold stars from the current attack affect the after action report. They can't be saved between attacks.

TCKA Alert	Punch Out Penalty
Green/Blue	Mild consequence
Yellow/Orange	Moderate consequence
Red	Severe consequence

Example: Dr. Laramie's Crew Vs. Mechaconga

It seemed like it would be a nice, quiet day for once in the Kaostopper office. But the Yellow Alert comes across the office's computer network, so Dr. Laramie, crack pilot "Lunchbox" McQuaid, and psychic Hybrid test subject Jenny Carpenter (played by Kat, Mesa, and Louise, respectively) hop in Lunchbox's helicopter and fly to Dallas to see what's going on. They need to get eyes on the kaiju leaving wreckage strewn across the Texas desert.

As GM, Lamar decides it's a Yellow Alert. There's definite evidence that Mechaconga attacked near Dallas but the mechakaiju is still nowhere in sight. That means three danger aspects will be in play. Lamar rolls Mechaconga's Terror at Good (+3) and his roll of a +1 gets it to Great (+4). Kat rolls Dr. Laramie's Kaiju Studies, Mesa rolls Lunchbox's Operate, and Louise rolls Jenny's Empathy. Kat keeps Dr. Laramie's Studies at Superb (+5), so she gets to declare the first danger aspect. Mechaconga hates displays of military might, so the first aspect is AIR BASE LOCKDOWN. Lamar decides to call back to a drinking contest the crew had with Caori Parker, an NPC kaiju Ace. He adds PARKER IS ON DUTY...AND DRUNK as the second danger aspect. The players get the last say and they defer to Louise, who rolled better than Mesa. She declares that Jenny can sense SOMEONE CLUTCHED IN THE GRIP OF MECHACONGA.

While the players discuss their plans, Lamar thinks about the scenes. He decides the AIR BASE LOCKDOWN is going to be a conflict between the players and the military over access that will let the players see a new fighter jet built with K-Tek. Parker needs to be convinced he should stand down, so that will require a contest. Finally, getting the civilian out of Mechaconga's grasp sounds like a challenge to anyone, even a well trained kaiju crew like his players.

The players decide to tackle the airbase first. Dr. Laramie and Jenny come face to face with General Rudolph, who doesn't want to admit the K-Tek jet even exists. The stakes for the conflict are set; Rudolph needs to be taken out to give the crew access. The conflict plays out with rolls of Provoke, Rapport, and Ambition between everyone. In the end, General Rudolph concedes but not before taking out Jenny. The General admits they summoned Mechaconga using an old radio frequency, thinking their new K-Tek jet could take it down. They didn't count on the beast snatching the jet out of midair! Mechaconga now carries the fighter jet (and its pilot trapped inside) in one of his giant mechanical mitts. The pilot can't eject with Mechaconga's mighty fingers wrapped around the cockpit. Jenny's display of her Hybrid-enhanced empathy intrigues the General, and Lamar decides that the General's inquiries with corporate about acquiring her as an asset will play out as a subplot in later sessions.

Meanwhile, Parker is stumbling around in his *batteboto* in a web of canyons. Lunchbox's chopper arrives on the scene. They can't get Parker to stand down over the radio, so Lunchbox appeals to the Ace's pride by issuing a challenge. If the Ace can't find Lunchbox's helicopter hiding in the canyons, he will be no good against Mechaconga. Parker agrees and the contest is on. Lunchbox succeeds with style on a roll during the contest, giving her a gold star for later use. Unfortunately, that's the only roll she succeeds at during the contest. Parker wins the contest with two out of three rolls. In the narrative, Parker wins as he locks onto Lunchbox's craft with a missile that would have blown the pilot out of the sky. Good thing this was just a friendly contest between friends!

The crew comes together when they get a call saying Mechaconga is heading for Dallas. Lunchbox's chopper buzzes the mechakaiju, which still has the K-Tek fighter jet firmly grasped in its hand. Mesa succeeds at a Pilot roll to get in close enough to see that the pilot is still alive. Dr. Laramie fails a Combat roll to damage Mechaconga's arm with the chopper's guns to free the pilot. Jenny reaches out with her mind and succeeds with style on an Operate roll to pull the eject lever on the fighter.

Looking back at the scenes, Lamar determines that the crew succeeded in getting into the airbase and rescuing the pilot, but failed at the canyon race against Parker. Two wins and one failure lowers the alert by one to a Blue Alert, which means if the players punch out and go home, they each suffer a mild consequence. Jenny and Lunchbox both have gold stars, so only Dr. Laramie suffers a mild consequence, which manifests as an **AWKWARD PHOTO OP** with the General.

VOGEL'S KAIJU RECOGNITION GUIDE, 7TH EDITION

When this guide began back in the 1950s, the world was a much different place. There weren't official kaiju lists or 24-hour news coverage. Magazines like *STOMP* and *Rubble Rouser* were decades away. Casual kaiju fans and *otakaiju* kept this guide alive for seven editions because of the quality of our coverage. We've been watching kaiju since there were only a few kaiju to watch. With this edition, we collect information on the top fifteen kaiju currently known to be alive. We hope our readers get close enough for a picture but stay far away enough to be able to develop it.

Look up!
Look out!

Ken E. Vogel, Jr.

AMANDA

Amanda began her career as a young intern at Monstersanto. But she wasn't just there to work for free and sling coffee. She was a Freezilly looking for some dirt on her employer. What she found was far, far greater. Nobody knows if the chemical spill was meant to kill her or scare her off the company's trail. It backfired, turning the kaiju activist into the very thing that she was trying to protect. Her time as a kaiju hasn't changed her idealism; she fights for fair treatment for kaiju not with petitions and boycotts but by knocking down factories and shouting the crimes of the corporations while she does it.

Amanda has no real powers beyond her size. She does possess above-average intelligence, which makes up for a lack of acid breath or hideous insect wings. Amanda's attacks are far more calculated and not the common rampages of other kaiju. She attacks factories to destroy output but minimizes danger to the employees. She also offers an additional challenge in the form of possibly being bad PR for both the company and the kaiju Ace sent to take her down. The public seems fine when robots brutally battle a monster. A fifty-foot woman, less so. She's more often subdued once the company she attacks heeds her demands or if someone talks her down from her current outrage.

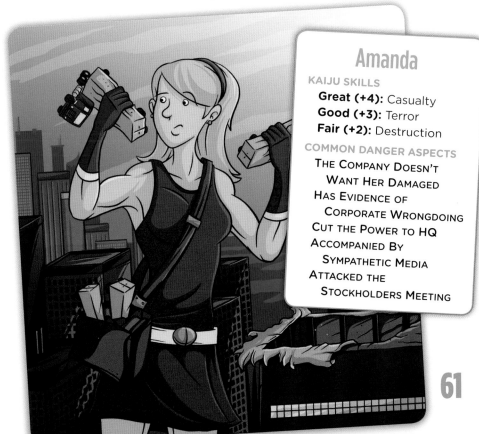

Amanda

KAIJU SKILLS

Great (+4): Casualty
Good (+3): Terror
Fair (+2): Destruction

COMMON DANGER ASPECTS

THE COMPANY DOESN'T WANT HER DAMAGED
HAS EVIDENCE OF CORPORATE WRONGDOING
CUT THE POWER TO HQ
ACCOMPANIED BY SYMPATHETIC MEDIA
ATTACKED THE STOCKHOLDERS MEETING

ANGINUS

Vampires may not exist, but this kaiju proves to be more terrifying than any stuffy old count or brooding immortal teen. The sound of a thumping heartbeat precedes Anginus just long enough for the people to become terrified. Then the monstrous, floating, throbbing heart appears and starts to pick up small snacks off the streets. It usually heads for highly populated areas and has shown a limited intelligence by attacking hospitals and bloodbanks. It can be beaten in a conventional manner but Anginus has shown it can't be destroyed. Even the smallest amount of contact with blood awakens the beast again and sets it on another rampage.

Anginus is a giant mutated floating heart. Its thumping heartbeat seems to be some form of communication; Anginus beats faster when angry, slower when subdued. The tentacles that spiral out from the beast are strong enough to smash buildings. There's an additional danger to any humans present; the tentacles are covered in thousands of sucking mouths, which can drain someone dry in a matter of seconds.

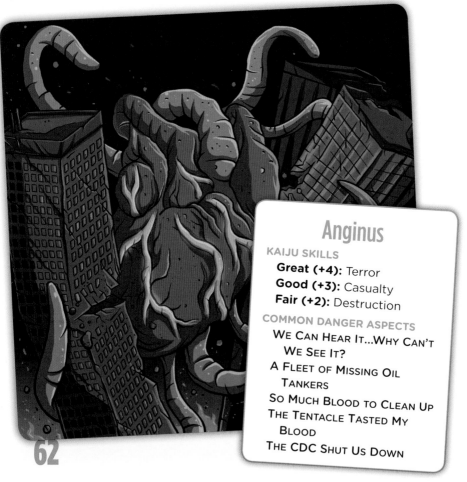

Anginus

KAIJU SKILLS

Great (+4): Terror
Good (+3): Casualty
Fair (+2): Destruction

COMMON DANGER ASPECTS

WE CAN HEAR IT...WHY CAN'T WE SEE IT?

A FLEET OF MISSING OIL TANKERS

SO MUCH BLOOD TO CLEAN UP

THE TENTACLE TASTED MY BLOOD

THE CDC SHUT US DOWN

BLOBSTERA

Vessels began to drift into ports along the Eastern Seaboard covered in a strange, amber-like coating. The ships were well preserved but anything inside not made of steel had disappeared. The amber vessels turned out to be the waste products of Blobstera. It was dissolving any organic material on the ships. Then, when it could no longer pull nutrition from the nodes, the ships broke off from Blobstera and drifted home.

Blobstera doesn't bite, chomp, or stomp. It absorbs. It forms pseudopods out of its strange pink mass and presses them against whatever it eats. Once the pink blob absorbs the object, specialized chemicals within the creature break it down. Fighting the beast becomes a challenge when you can't hurt it but it can hurt you.

Blobstera

KAIJU SKILLS
- **Great (+4):** Terror
- **Good (+3):** Casualty
- **Fair (+2):** Destruction

COMMON DANGER ASPECTS
- SMALLER PIECES KEEP FIGHTING
- UNBREAKABLE SKIN
- THE ACE IS ALIVE INSIDE BLOBSTERA
- EATING AWAY AT SUPPORT BEAMS
- WE NEED TO MOP UP EVERY DROP

GAHZONGA

Current theory places kaiju as a recent phenomena. Gahzonga, however, calls that theory into question. The kaiju first arose during a volcanic eruption on the Big Island of Hawai'i. The creature bears a striking resemblance to an obscure volcanic deity, and it has attracted new fanatics. Whether this is the same creature depicted in cave drawings or a kaiju that just happened to fit the name and motive is as yet undetermined.

Gahzonga's rock hard skin and massive strength make it a challenge for any kaiju Ace. More devastating is the beast's method of travel. It moves under the surface using lava tubes and fractures in the Earth's crust. Not only must crews deal with the monster, they have to slow down spontaneous volcanic eruptions caused by the kaiju busting through the crust. The creature is immune to the magma but loves to spread it around when it attacks.

Gahzonga

KAIJU SKILLS

Great (+4): Destruction
Good (+3): Casualty
Fair (+2): Terror

COMMON DANGER ASPECTS

STOP THAT LAVA FLOW!
FANATICS TOOK A SACRIFICE
MAGMA BURNING THROUGH THE ROOF
IT'S EMITTING NOXIOUS GASES
GAHZONGA CHUNK EMBEDDED IN THE REACTOR CORE

GATCHAMANERA

This kaiju was the subject of an early Kaijumoto public relations campaign. The company rolled out a press tour claiming this was a kaiju that everyone could love. Kids watched the Saturday morning cartoon. Adults could get pictures taken on the creature's back. The secret to the company's success was a K-Tek helmet that let a specially trained handler control the beast. When the helmet went missing and the handler turned up dead, Gatchamanera struck out on his own.

The kaiju's turtle genetics give it a massive shell that's impenetrable to conventional weapons. The magnetic field generators strapped to its legs can be used to fly and fire focused electromagnetic beams that can shut down most modern technology. If the control helmet is ever located or re-engineered, it could be used to try and reason with the beast, who has been shown to have a childlike personality. A trained counselor can bring Gatchamanera in for a soft landing and easy transport back to a kaiju holding facility. Upset the poor thing and its tantrum can level a mountain.

Gatchamanera

KAIJU SKILLS

Great (+4): Destruction, Casualty
Average (+1): Terror

COMMON DANGER ASPECTS

WE JUST NEED ONE RARE PART TO FIX THE HELMET

EVERYTHING WE THROW AT IT BOUNCES OFF THAT SHELL

IT'S SHUTTING DOWN ELECTRONICS IN A TWO-MILE RADIUS

HOVERING OUT OF RANGE

AN OTAKAIJU BUILT A NEW HELMET

65

GYROS

Tornadoes are destructive enough, but when there's a kaiju causing the wind they become ten times worse. A mysterious tornado hit multiple kaiju corporation assets throughout the Midwest, with no discernable—or natural—pattern. Once the storm starting hitting places outside of Tornado Alley, crews were put on high alert. Gyros brings the destruction of a massive windstorm to urban areas powered by the intelligence of a creature that somehow senses when kaiju are captured or in pain. Gyros wants all kaiju to be free and does its best to help.

The center of the windstorm is powered by a long purple serpent that stretches for miles. Gyros can spin with the intensity of a jet engine and cause massive storm winds to whip up in moments. Most Aces have little problem defeating the monster in a straight up battle, but getting through the massive winds and wreckage caused by the storm is the real challenge.

Gyros

KAIJU SKILLS

Superb (+5): Destruction
Fair (+2): Terror, Casualty

COMMON DANGER ASPECTS

200 MPH WINDS
HURRICANE IN A JUNKYARD
QUICKLY WHIPPING TAIL
NEWS TEAM CAUGHT IN
THE STORM
CAN'T HEAR MY CREW
OVER THE ROAR

KALGON

Sometimes K-Tek's intentions backfire spectacularly. Kalgon was a relatively harmless kaiju that was the test subject of a Hawkesbury Array Restraint Obstruction Laser Device. The material in the restraints was built to contract whenever Kalgon did something against the wishes of its masters. What the designers didn't anticipate was the metal in the chains being absorbed into Kalgon and giving it control of the laser drones meant to observe the kaiju.

It's hard to choose what's most dangerous about Kalgon. The creature's mouths bite and scream as it floats through the air. Its hundreds of eyes let it survey the situation from every angle, making traps and ambushes hard to pull off. The K-Tek harness that it wears provides it with floating orbs that deliver searing laser blasts to anything that threatens the beast.

Kalgon

KAIJU SKILLS

Superb (+5): Casualty

Fair (+2): Destruction, Terror

COMMON DANGER ASPECTS

WEB OF DEADLY LASERS

LASHING CHAINS SMASHED THE HOSPITAL

CAN WE REBOOT THE HARNESS TO CONTROL IT?

HOVERING IN A SNIPER SPOT

BURNED A HOLE THROUGH THE BATTEBOTO'S HEAD

KUDZUS

San Francisco first felt the wrath of this plant-like kaiju. The original Kudzus is dead and gone, burned in the great San Francisio Fire of '67. Its spores still remain, occasionally spawning a new version when they find the right conditions to grow. Kudzus grows to great heights in the span of a few hours. It prefers to attack cities with a high yearly rainfall, such as Seattle or New Orleans. The Monstersanto chain Saladaze profits from using ethically farmed Kudzus leaves in its meals, and restricts its sale to other franchises.

The plant DNA inside Kudzus gives it amazing regenerative powers. Severed limbs regrow in a matter of minutes. Aces have damaged the head only for the body to fight on. Keeping the head separated will kill the beast eventually but the Ace has to keep it away from the grasping hands of the body for several minutes. It is also weak to fire and dry or cold conditions. Successive growths retain a sense of memory from previous generations, so luring the Kudzus into the same trap a second time often proves difficult.

Kudzus

KAIJU SKILLS
Great (+4): Destruction, Casualty
Average (+1): Terror

COMMON DANGER ASPECTS
POORLY-TIMED THUNDERSTORM
IT'S WEARING THAT BUILDING LIKE A SHELL
LASERS BLAZING EVERYWHERE
RIGHT FERTILIZER TRUCK, WRONG TIME
A KUDZUS SAPLING GROWS IN BROOKLYN

MECHACONGA

The first of Z-Wave's automated *batteboto*. It was built to defeat Queen Conga and display the advanced robotic intelligence that Z-Wave's scientists would use to revolutionize kaiju defense. The scientists succeeded too well. Upon seeing Queen Conga, Mechaconga recognized her as the one worthy mate in this world and convinced her to run away with him. *Otakaiju* gossip magazines like *STOMP* spill a lot of ink over whether or not the couple remains together.

Mechaconga is a giant robot built to look like an ape. Golden shoulder panels convert the sun's rays to power the machine. The energy can also be focused out of Mechaconga's eyes into a devastating laser blast. The banana-shaped decorations on his belt are in fact missiles, grenades, and explosive devices that further confound Aces trying to defeat the beast. Aces report that sometimes Mechaconga gets a crush on a *batteboto*, which causes a couple of awkward complications to arise. Either Mechaconga tries to initiate mating rituals, or Queen Conga arrives ready to fight for Mechaconga's love.

Mechaconga

KAIJU SKILLS

Good (+3): Destruction, Terror, Casualty

COMMON DANGER ASPECTS

JEALOUS RAGE

CAUGHT AN AIRPLANE BY THE TAIL

THE MILITARY WANTS TO KEEP MECHACONGA FOR ITSELF

GUYS, THIS BANANA IS NUCLEAR

MUST BE BATTEBOTO MATING SEASON

MECHATHOR

The second of Z-Wave's attempts at a mechakaiju deterrent, Mechathor uses a biolelectric generator made from cloned parts of another kaiju, Thorzilla. Mechathor and Thorzilla despise each other in a way that only siblings truly can. Mechathor adheres to its programming for the most part to protect cities, it's just exceedingly bad at its job.

The electric warhammer it wields bleeds energy everywhere. The lightest touch sets off multiple energy strikes, which often cause blackouts and radical shifts to Mechathor's programming. Much of the destruction caused by this kaiju is electromagnetic pulse-style frying of electronics. Kaiju companies that fail to stop Mechathor often end up shelling out to replace everything from smartphones to vehicle computer chips.

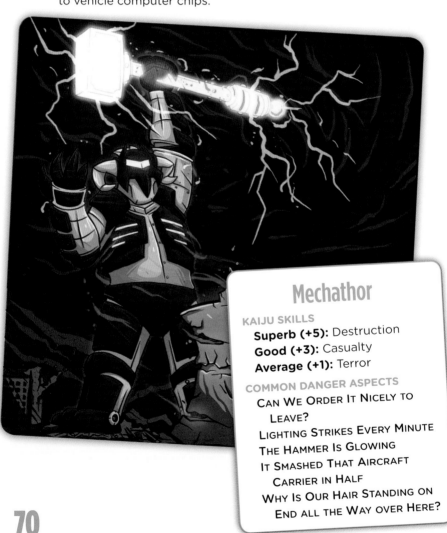

Mechathor

KAIJU SKILLS

Superb (+5): Destruction
Good (+3): Casualty
Average (+1): Terror

COMMON DANGER ASPECTS

CAN WE ORDER IT NICELY TO LEAVE?
LIGHTING STRIKES EVERY MINUTE
THE HAMMER IS GLOWING
IT SMASHED THAT AIRCRAFT CARRIER IN HALF
WHY IS OUR HAIR STANDING ON END ALL THE WAY OVER HERE?

MOTHBALLARA

Mothballara is one of the kaiju with the most storied careers. It appeared shortly after Daikaiju's attack and regularly reappears around the world. Scientists think that every successive showing has been a different Mothballara due to subtle differences in the wing patterns and slight modulation of its death call. GWAI Group recently introduced a smartphone that uses Mothballara's death call as a message notification. It really puts people on edge.

The death call is a sonic attack that shatters windows and knocks military vehicles aside like toys. The beast's wings allow it to fly at jetfighter speeds and generate winds strong enough to push over *batteboto*. Mothballara's eyes can also flash to blind opponents just long enough for it to attack with a large stinger that easily punctures thick steel armor. Finally, the creature leaves behind glowing spheres in its flight path. The spheres emit a noxious, foul-smelling radioactive fog when they break, but "mothball bombs" are widely prized on the otakaiju black market if found intact.

Mothballara

KAIJU SKILLS

Good (+3): Destruction, Terror, Casualty

COMMON DANGER ASPECTS

HERE COMES THE GUSTS
DEAFENING SONIC DEATH CALL
BLINDED BY THE LIGHT
STINGER SPIKED THE MAYOR'S CAR
UNEXPLODED MOTHBALL BOMBS HIDDEN EVERYWHERE

QUEEN CONGA

Her majesty was discovered on a jungle island in Southeast Asia by filmmakers in 1971, where she was attended to by a cargo cult on the island. The giant crate used as her altar gave the expedition the idea that she may have been moved from somewhere else. Unlike many of her contemporaries, she came to Menagerie Island willingly, possibly to find a mate. However, when she was sold to New York, she learned humans could never be trusted and went off to conquer her own kingdoms.

Queen Conga has all the features of a giant ape. Scientists estimate her intelligence at near human levels and she can out-ma-neuver kaiju Aces with her ability to jump from skyscraper to skyscraper like trees in the forest. She knows if she takes a hostage along for the ride she makes it more difficult for the humans to hurt her, so she usually picks up some poor unsuspecting tourist and sticks them in the band of her crown during her rampage.

Queen Conga

KAIJU SKILLS

Great (+4): Casualty
Good (+3): Terror
Fair (+2): Destruction

COMMON DANGER ASPECTS

I Went to High School With That Hostage
Dancing on Top of the Building
Peeling That Bus Like a Banana
Her Crown Seems to Be Missing
Not Letting Go of That Airplane Anytime Soon

QUEEN GHIRODELLORA

The other queen of the kaiju confounds those looking to classify these monsters solely as a natural phenomenon. Her angelic form points to being man-made, and she possesses some form of basic intelligence, but no corporation has come forth to claim responsibility. Her form also has a sleekness to it the mechakaiju lack. If she was manufactured, it was by an intelligence far beyond our own, using technology that K-Tek has yet to unlock.

Ghirodellora's power comes from the strange gems embedded in her body, which blaze with a sinister red light. She can fire vicious laser blasts from any one of the gems, but usually generates a red shield from those in her hands. She has giant golden wings, used for mobility and flight. When defeated, all that remains after a flash of golden light are the four gems, which lie dormant until whatever causes her to awaken happens again, in another eruption of light.

Queen Ghirodellora

KAIJU SKILLS

Good (+3): Destruction, Terror, Casualty

COMMON DANGER ASPECTS

STEPPING ON PUNY HUMANS

WHY IS SHE ONLY BLASTING SOLDIERS?

SHE SEEMS TO BE PROTECTING THAT BUILDING

FLYING INTO THE STRATOSPHERE

THE KAIJU MUSEUM IS UNDER ATTACK

RADON

For many years, kaiju corporations claimed their processes were clean and safe. Kaiju are natural, so any products made from them are, by their nature, also natural. When Radon first appeared, it wasn't even classified as a kaiju. The beast made its presence known in Minsk by dissolving an entire factory in minutes. The corporations don't like to talk about Radon. While most kaiju get top coverage, Radon attacks are usually downplayed for some unknown reason.

Radon is a sentient cloud of toxic gas. It is able to adjust its composition from harmless vapor to acidic cloud on the fly, even adjusting parts to be different consistencies. The cloud maintains a monster-like face when it moves. It is difficult to fight in a conventional manner, so it is usually contained or dispersed with large fans or other devices. Radon often appears around corporate manufacturing areas.

Radon

KAIJU SKILLS

Great (+4): Destruction, Terror
Average (+1): Casualty

COMMON DANGER ASPECTS

WE DON'T HAVE ENOUGH GAS MASKS

THERE'S A HOLE IN THE CONTAINMENT SUIT

CAN WE MAKE IT TO THE AIR CONDITIONER FACTORY?

SEAL UP ALL THE WINDOWS AND DOORS IN THIS BUILDING

WE NEED TO BUILD A BIGGER FAN

THORZILLA

This kaiju introduced the terror of giant monsters to Europe. Clad in ancient glacial ice, Thorzilla nearly shattered the iron curtain with its subzero breath. The beast has since been seen nearly all around the world, through very rarely near the equator. The heat might be a natural weakness of the beast or it might know that many kaiju already claim warmer climates as their turf.

Thorzilla is a large horned lizard covered in patches of ancient glacial ice that act as armor. It freezes opponents with a breath attack, then smashes them to pieces with a headbutt from its horns. The creature also generates a massive bioelectric field, which makes it a deadly opponent when encountered near water.

Thorzilla

KAIJU SKILLS

Great (+4): Destruction
Good (+3): Casualty
Fair (+2): Terror

COMMON DANGER ASPECTS

THE PORT IS ELECTRIFIED
OVERTURNED SHIP IN THE HARBOR
TURNED THE HIGHWAY INTO AN ICE RINK
BATTEBOTO'S FEET ARE FROZEN TO THE GROUND
THE PRESIDENT IS ENCASED IN ICE

75

MEGAYEN MAGAZINE KAIJUCO PROFILES

Investors looking for a solid return need look no further than kaiju consumer product corporations. Fads like *Monster Patch Kids* and *Adolescent Retrofrog Ninjavirus* may come and go, but these companies have diversified beyond their traditional markets of military hardware and kids toys. K-Tek makes our lives easier every day by using the natural bounty of the kaiju harvest. Kaiju are a resource not going away any time soon, so investors looking to turn a human-sized nest egg into a kaiju-sized windfall should look into buying stock in one of the top five companies.

GWAI GROUP

Our top recommendation is the newest kaiju corporation, which does a lot to cultivate an air of mystery around itself. The dust had just settled from the shake-up that tore apart Z-Wave. Much of what remained was absorbed into Babayagich Corporation and it seemed that there would be a status quo of four kaiju corporations again. GWAI Group appeared just a few years ago with aggressive moves into markets dominated by competitors. Before long, investors started calling the sector the Big Five and GWAI Group was here to stay.

David Fan Fu is out of place compared to the other CEOs of kaiju corporations. He lacks the bluntness of Hawkesbury's Mary Bennett. He doesn't have the easy stage presence of Monstersanto's Tyrone Hartman. Mr. Fan Fu wants his company's performance to do the talking for him. And so far, GWAI Group has had plenty to say. Investors recognize his soft-spoken voice on earnings calls because when he does talk, what he says is important.

Beijing's roar into the world market was led by GWAI Group's attack on the kaiju market. The city still wants to be known as an industrial powerhouse but is no longer content with being a small sticker on the back of a product. They've given GWAI Group every advantage in regulations and tax breaks. GWAI group's manufacturing output has amplified Beijing's pollution problem. Newscast weather segments include the exact type and color of the smog every day. Yet since GWAI Group came to power, the city has suffered the least amount of damage from kaiju attacks than any major world city, thanks to the corporation's security methods. This is a source of pride for many citizens and a strength other corporations can't ignore.

The main offices of GWAI Group occupy most of a single tower known for a KaijuScope screen that runs the length and width of the building. KaijuScope electronics led the company's entry into the marketplace and the screen surpasses the hustle and bustle of anything in Tokyo or New York. Images cut through the choking, toxic fog as crystal clear as though they were in an electronics store window. Rumors are that the company is planning on using this as the focal point of this year's KaijuScope TV campaign rather than play to environmental interests to reduce the pollution.

GWAI Group's main push into new kaiju markets comes through Biwa Biotech. They're looking to lower medical costs by using kaiju

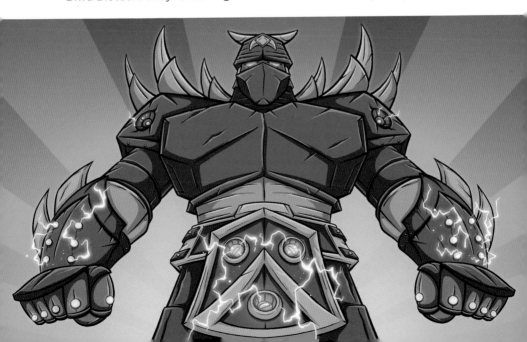

biomatter as the basis for new drugs and treatments. Genetically modified soldiers pop up from time to time but no company has yet to unlock the right code without the sort of side effects that end with goo-smeared walls and a series of payoffs and regrettable, accidental fires. Biwa Biotech is able to use these missteps to keep their corporate masters happy, which keeps the money flowing.

The one big step that GWAI Group took to announce its presence to the world was to station *Terracotta Ocean* in the Forbidden City for a week before it went public. The *batteboto* has been stationed there ever since, ready to protect the symbolic heart of China. Other GWAI Group *batteboto* have seen action, like *Terracotta Staff*'s two-day duel with Gahzonga, which received over three-million views on KaiTube. The *Terracotta* series of robots protect China from kaiju and have only made a few steps outside the homeland to intercept inbound monsters.

Despite the brand name, the *Terracotta* series is built with strong Yangtse steel from the company of the same name. GWAI Group's in-house design firm works on-site at the foundry. Rumors persist that the next series of robots will be the first to fashion *batteboto* after non-human forms. The designers supposedly had animals shipped on-site from the Beijing Zoo to study movement, attack, and defense for their designs. These rumors may also have been started to distract from the *Monster Dump* article that said the steel plant was one of the most unsafe places to work in the world.

The first major hit for Biwa Biotech that can be publicly acknowledged is its Blue Heaven enhancement supplements, in direct competition against Kaijumoto Keiretsu's Kaijumojo pills. In a lovely bit of corporate synergy, the commercials feature two men scaling the GWAI Group tower. One man pops a Blue Heaven and starts up the wall. The other, who looks suspiciously like a younger version of Artemis Kaneda, does not. The first man climbs up the tower easily, while the other man struggles. As they both near the top, the Kaneda look-alike loses his grip and falls. He lands below in a pile of cheap toy packaging, the logos of which are slyly similar to Kaijumoto's. It's not a subtle metaphor but it's made Blue Heaven a top seller in gas stations and drug stores across the world.

GWAI Group keeps its kaiju Aces out of the public eye. When they do appear, they wear polished chrome helmets and jumpsuits that only differ by color. The media coined a name for each, assigning a different element to each color. The most popular of the Terracotta Five is the blue-suited Mr. Water. All of the Terracotta Five are referred to as "Mister" regardless of outward appearances. The pilots prefer to speak by whispering something in the ear of someone in their entourage and have that person speak to the press. *Otakaiju* have theories about the identities of the pilots, even going to far to suggest that Dino Solomon not only is in charge of the program, but may have been piloting *Terracotta Sabbath* when it recently faced Anginus.

MONSTERSANTO

Our second best investment rose to prominence in the 1980s when it pioneered the release of kaiju consumer products. Most kaiju corporations limited themselves to military and industrial applications during the 1970s. Monstersanto rolled out consumer products that lit a fire under everyone to have a piece of a monster. While its lineage traces back to Starr Industries, Monstersanto doesn't dwell in the past like the other members of the kaiju corporation old guard. The company was the first to stop seeing kaiju as a problem and start seeing them as a solution.

Tyrone Hartman shocked the world when he made the call to change the way Monstersanto did business. He was a junior executive in the mid-1980s when he led the team that explored consumer kaiju projects. His successes propelled him to the CEO chair of Monstersanto in the year 2000. Despite a rocky economy and backlash from customers claiming strange side effects from foodstuffs like Dai-Donuts, Hartman has kept Monstersanto in the hearts and minds of the American people. And, most importantly, in their bellies and their wallets. Every Dai-Burger has a picture of Tyrone smiling down on the customers above the counter as if he's taking their order personally.

The nation's capital has been home to Monstersanto since Conga Eve. DC is a natural home for the company since it needs to lobby for advantageous regulations that help the company domestically, while throwing obstacles for other companies hoping to expand into the US. Washington has yet to suffer a major kaiju attack, but

MONSTERSANTO

Monstersanto's presence makes citizens feel safe. Whether it's the retractable dome armor on the Capitol Building or the massive robot *Teenage Death Lincoln* parked on the National Mall in an act of eternal vigilance, the company repays government loyalty with an excellent display of security.

Unlike most of the other kaiju corporations, Monstersanto's offices are open to the public. The entire first floor is a shopping mall dedicated to Monstersanto's most popular products as well as a test bed for new ideas that are being considered to roll out to the public. Flagship stores for brands like Dai-Burger, Nose Art, and Beauty/Monster get exclusive products that bring just as many tourists as the stodgy old monuments do.

Most of the company's top secret projects get developed directly at the Pentagon. Many of the old holdouts from Starr Industries that didn't want to give up making guns and armor work at the offices here. The US still has a lot of defense contracts with Monstersanto, most of which provide support for the regular military like kaiju foodstuffs and K-Tek medical equipment. The company has been trying to move into the hybrid soldier market with the hopes of signing new contracts that more directly align with the company's current direction.

Munroe Munitions is tied closely to the US Army but it also spends a lot of time researching what weaponry is most effective against kaiju. Rather than build the weapons on their own, they often subcontract manufacturing out to other companies. Most *batteboto* have at least one weapons system designed by Munroe. The main source of its profits are selling weaponry to state troopers and law enforcement. Munroe branded the weapons as necessary for kaiju defense until an Ace arrives on the scene, but it's mostly a way to convince cities to leave room in their budgets for unnecessary military-grade equipment. A Munroe TacTech automobile will be crushed by Gahzonga's claw just as easily as a regular-priced police cruiser.

Lincoln Lasertech is responsible for keeping Monstersanto *batteboto* up and running. *Teenage Death Lincoln* is still one of Monstersanto's most popular creations, even if the company wants to get out of making giant robots. Years of replacing the robot's eyes after kaiju battles has diversified laser technology, allowing it to be used for personal defense and in the home. Purchasers of the popular Lasertech Laserwebs home defense systems can now choose between non-lethal (alerts the local authorities to a break-in) and lethal (creates a web of beams that will cut and burn trespassers, only available in some states).

Dai-Burger stands as Monstersanto's most popular brand. Despite consumers shifting to healthier options, the public still wants their CongaBurgers and full rack of Patriot Fries. Hartman laughed off accusations of addictive additives at a congressional hearing last year, but every few months another viral video or picture of what the food is really made of gives the marketing team a new headache. Monstersanto's most recent ad campaign shows a kaiju rising up from the water. Behind the counters, the burger slingers flip switches on their registers. Each of the restaurants takes off and forms a giant *batteboto* to defeat the monster. The ad makes a pretty clear connection—spend money at a Dai-Burger and you're fighting kaiju while you eat.

Bobbi Lee Gentry won last season's *Monstersanto Presents America's Next Top Kaiju Ace* reality competition. Her combination of telegenic energy and physical fitness made her an early favorite to win the competition. She had some dramatic clashes with fellow contestant Rich Norris over whether women were suitable for the role of kaiju Ace. Her subsequent rescue of Norris during the siege of Chicago turned the season finale into a must-watch blockbuster. It solidified her as a role model for little girls everywhere wanting to climb into a *batteboto* of their own one day. Though she's seen less kaiju action than other Aces, she's not the first to be more popular based on personality than battle record. The American people love her and her *batteboto*, *Chihuahua Chupacabra*, and her country album just went platinum.

KAIJUMOTO KEIRETSU

The grand dame of the kaiju consumer products industry still brings in the most sales of all the companies profiled here. The general public identifies kaiju products with Kaijumoto Keiretsu in the same way that people call adhesive bandages Band-Aids or facial tissue Kleenex. They created an entire industry in the 1970s and still lead it in many ways. This company stands tall after all its competitors in the Pacific Rim faded away from decades of kaiju appearances. So long as there's been a public hungry for products made from kaiju bone and kaiju leather, there's been Kaijumoto Keiretsu.

Kaijumoto's structure as a conglomerate of several companies offers regular changes in leadership by rotating Chief Executive Officers. A new CEO is appointed every five years from the leaders of the *keiretsu*. Madoka Kokuchi currently sits atop Kaijumoto. Her time in the top spot has returned Kaijumoto to a more traditional means of production, in contrast with the old CEO's Western-friendly ideas. She took over for Artemis Kaneda, the son of Dr. Hideo Kaneda last year. Kokuchi won her position easily after Kaneda's disastrous investment of both company and personal resources in the box-office bomb *Tokugawa vs. Blobstera*, an alternate history science-fiction film that detailed what would have happened if kaiju arrived during the Warring States period of Japan's history.

Osaka stands as a symbol of Japan's ability to withstand kaiju attacks. The city has been hit several times over the years and rebuilds within months. Most local kaiju recovery programs are modeled after the Osaka Recovery Corps. The Corps is a fertile recruitment ground for kaiju companies looking to bolster their security and emergency planning. Many Kaijumoto crew members have worn the distinctive white hard hats of the ORC or been trained by one of their members. Thanks to technology advances, the white hard hats are now more symbolic than functional, but members display them with pride in their daily lives in between kaiju attacks.

Osaka Castle is synonymous with the company. Kaijumoto's most famous ad campaign featured time-lapse photography of a devastated city being rebuilt up from behind the castle. Despite the many attacks that have hit the city, the castle has never fallen. Other landmarks around the world have been trashed multiple times; the current record holder is the Golden Gate Bridge. Osaka Castle is a source of pride for the country. The company capitalizes on that pride by featuring the castle in some way, shape, or form in every visual ad it produces. The brushstrokes of Kaijumoto's kanji-style logo are based on an artist's impression of the castle's main tower.

The factories of Yamato Robotics are legendary for their efficiency and design. Robots build robots for building robots. Kaijumoto robots exist in factories around the world, even direct competitors.

No other company provides the precision needed for working with kaiju materials. Many a child first found a love of science and engineering with Yamato Roblox building kits. Each box of Blox comes with an ID badge that, if presented at a Yamato facility, allows the child a free tour (accompanied by an adult). All Yamato facilities have small gift shops to sell more Roblox toys directly.

Kitayama Chemicals represents Kaijuimoto's entry into consumer products. They are the power behind Faraday Kosmetics, which introduced kaiju musk cologne and kaiju acne cream to the market. Anyone with a teenager at home knows the overpowering smell of Faraday's Atomik.

Kaijumoto's most popular product these days is the K-Onnekt smartphone. It's made for *otakaiju* who want to make sure they're following their favorite monsters all day, every day. It comes with a high-resolution camera optimized for Monstergram to catch a kaiju in the act. The phone synchronizes with the user's social media account to automatically post everything. It comes with the widest selection of authentic kaiju calls for use as ringers, notifications, and other tones. The audio is so realistic, the commercials feature a kaiju fan accidentally attracting multiple kaiju with his ringtones. They all have a big laugh and then fight each other as the kid escapes.

The company's star kaiju Ace embodies his company like few others. Hanzo "Tiger" Tora doesn't give press conferences. He doesn't do commercials or public appearances outside of charity events sponsored by Kaijimoto. There's a rugged quality to the scars across his face that gave him his nickname. Nearly every kid in Japan owns a model of *Perfect Empty*, Hanzo's *batteboto* that still stands to this day. Other Aces soak up the glory and celebrity after climbing out of the cockpit. Hanzo walks silently through a sea of respectful journalists waiting for him to say a single world about the defeated beast.

KAIJUMOTO
KEIRETSU

HAWKESBURY LIMITED

Australia existed as the heart of the *batteboto* industry for many years. It was a prime location for the first manufacturing plants, with Western-friendly governments along with an industrial base able to build the *boto*'s massive armored shells. Company founder Montgomery Hawkesbury was fascinated with the kaiju, devoting much of his life and resources to their study. He rivaled Dr. Kaneda as the world's foremost expert on kaiju, taking a more direct approach that yielded different results than Kaneda's clinical studies. Though mourned for his heroic death during the Lost Valley incident, his critics never neglect to mention his distasteful reputation as a hunting enthusiast. His development of robozoids was also met mixed reviews—a boon for industry but weapons in the hands of the rich on safari. He was a complicated and ultimately tragic figure.

Mary T.T. Bennett struggles to get out from the large shadow of the company's founder. Bennett likes to say her company works with kaiju rather than exploiting them. Her press conferences usually include some anecdote of wisdom imparted by Montgomery. Critics of her say that if Ol' Monty actually said all those things Bennett quotes, he would still be around to say them.

Bennett's first move to make her own legacy was moving the main offices of Hawkesbury from Melbourne to Canberra. The move to Canberra allowed the corporation easier access to government contacts and policy makers, but also came as a wave of kaiju rights advocacy swept the nation. Protests in Sydney may signal an impending PR problem for Hawkesbury.

The kaiju defense batteries built to protect Parliament House only recently went online. Higher profile cities like Sydney and Melbourne have suffered multiple attacks but Canberra is still untouched as of this writing. Some in the opposing party complain about the cost of building these defenses. Hawkesbury officials usually reply with kaiju statistics and a veiled reminder of how little the government pays for such thorough protection.

Many of Hawkesbury's products feature some component of Thorzilla, one of the first kaiju Montgomery Hawkesbury personally captured. Hanging Rock Concrete manufacturers the most famous of these products, Thorcrete, which is a godsend for companies looking to rebuild quickly after kaiju attacks. When the compound is kept under extreme cold and pressure, it stays in a liquid form. It sprays like an insulating foam but when it hardens, it rivals concrete for load bearing and hardiness. It has a limited use in areas where winters are harsh, but many, if not all of the buildings located along the Pacific Rim have major portions rebuilt with Thorcrete.

Not only does Hanging Rock Concrete use kaiju-based chemicals to provide stronger support for buildings, it also doubles as a *batteboto* and robozoid pilot testing ground. The company began as an example of how robozoids could be used for industrial purposes, and also acquired a few surplus *batteboto* during the downfall of Z-Wave that were converted to industrial work. Many top pilots rose up from the ranks of factory workers. Hanging Rock remains one of the few places a civilian can get stick time without signing on for a military hitch or graduating from a prestigious piloting academy.

Another of Hawkesbury's ventures, Florey Pharmaceuticals, began as a shifty front for the various snake oils and other patent medicines offered as part of Z-Wave's expansion out of the useless electronics department. Hawkesbury acquired the brand when Z-Wave folded and has spent the past decade rehabilitating it into a name that people think of when they need a little chemical assistance. The only product still being produced from the old days is an over-the-counter sedative strong enough to let people sleep through a kaiju attack. Z-Wave never quite knew what to do with the formula, but a quick rebranding as Tocka-Doze made Florey the top pharmaceutical firm in the world.

The media often wonders if Ace Clive Dandridge's ego is bigger than his *batteboto*. Dandridge came out of Hanging Rock Concrete with one of the few Z-Wave cast-offs still able to handle active service. *Sweet Molly Scrapper* may not look like much, but she (Dandridge has punched reporters for calling the robot "it") stays in the fight far longer that others of her age or construction. Dandridge's battles aren't pretty, due to his strategy of letting Molly take a beating and then striking when the kaiju's fatigue sets in. Clive doesn't have a handsome face and can't give an interview without a heavy edit from the censors, but his working class bravado means that no matter what bar he walks into around the world, the first round (and many to follow) is not on him.

BABAYAGITCH CORPORATION

The fall of Z-Wave was barely over before the rise of Babayagitch began. A group of Russian businessmen representing an oil conglomerate and several different countries from the old Soviet Union snapped up Z-Wave assets through means both legal and not. The company entered the kaiju business with very little in the way of actual kaiju assets. Their inexpensive products and heavy marketing have changed that, but they are still known as a kaiju corporation with only one kaiju on their side: Babushka.

Ludmilla Babayagitch, called Babushka by her employees, has all the destruction, terror, and casualty of a kaiju compacted down into the five-foot frame of a ninety-year-old woman. Her company rewards loyalty and brutally punishes failure. She is unerringly polite when seen in the public, but ask anyone who has sat across from her at a negotiating table or had to explain a downturn in profits and they'll tell a story as harrowing as dangling from a gargoyle during a kaiju rampage.

Moscow is where the Babayagitch corporation hangs its furry hat. Many of the buildings the company uses were once government buildings, all concrete sides and dank, dark twisting basements that were leased to the company in exchange for sharing Z-Wave's K-Tek devices. Working here is the exact opposite of the glass cubicles and pinball machines that start-ups love to advertise. Ludmilla Babayagitch claims that money not spent on office renewals is money spent on the things that matter to a company—employees. According to inside sources, Babayagitch employees make 150% of what their equivalent positions in other companies make. A lot of employees are willing to put up with the weird noises (and even weirder smells) inside the buildings to go home to a much nicer apartment.

BABAYAGITCH
CORPORATION

The Kremlin looks more secure now than it did during the height of the Cold War. Concrete walls and active patrols do much to cultivate an air of security, but the return of an old tradition does more to show how Babayagitch has climbed into the top of the kaiju corporations. The past few years have featured *batteboto* parades in Red Square. Lesser parades only feature kaiju Aces and their *boto* from the home team, but for important days, Aces come together from around the world. The 50th anniversary of Daikaiju day featured *boto* from all the major corporations walking in the parade, with only a few incidents between the pilots.

Dostayevsky Shipyard was one of the few places in the world big enough to keep its original purpose of building ships and also convert facilities to manufacture *batteboto*. The crossover of naval and kaiju worlds gave rise to unusual superstitions about the machines built here. *Boto* must be christened with a bottle of vodka from a local distillery, or be subject to superstitions of being horribly mangled and mutilated by kaiju. Ships from the yard are named for kaiju. The legend on the docks is that when a ship named for a kaiju goes offline, the namesake will show up for an attack soon.

WHAT IS BABAYAGITCH HIDING?

Much of the Mechathor project ended up at the feet of Karpov Cryogenics. There were some good innovations made by the designers that were lost in the terrible release of the project. The company has since proven to be one of the corporation's most profitable. In return, Ludmilla Babayagitch allowed the executive vice president to slowly reassemble the team that built Mechathor. They've convinced Ludmilla that the third time is the charm and hope to roll out Mechababa within the next few years.

The oil conglomerate that first created Babayagitch rebranded as Gazpew Energy, seeking solutions for the energy market coming from the kaiju. The company is one of the few within any of the kaiju corporations looking into the origins of the kaiju. Discovering where the monsters come from could mean harnessing the energy that makes kaiju and turning it into energy that can power homes and industries. The company most recently announced plans for the Egg, a hybrid vehicle that runs on gasoline and a proprietary fuel known only as Kaiju Oil.

The JPhone pulled Babayagitch out of obscurity and into people's pockets. A middling phone technologically, the company took a bite out of the market with dozens of customization options from decorative to technical. JPhone options can also be easily switched, so a phone based on Mothballara's color scheme one day can look like Radon the next. The data plans are also just as modular, making it a way for low-income families to enjoy a bit of luxury.

Katerina Black was one of a few thousand people in the audience when Gahzonga attacked London's Wembley Stadium during a rock concert. Amid the chaos, she climbed into a damaged *batteboto* and fought the creature to a standstill. Babayagitch hired her straight out of the hospital and built a new robot, *Orphan Widow*, for her to use. Rumors claim that Katerina and Ludmilla are very close and that if something happened to one, the other would be inconsolable. Considering one has a giant robot with ten kaiju kills under its belt and the other is the head of one of the largest corporations in the world, those two have the most secure jobs in the world.

READY FOR A PROMOTION?
Run your own kaiju corporation with the card game!

KAIJU INCORPORATED
THE CARD GAME OF MONSTER PROFITS

ERIC B. VOGEL
CHRIS RUGGIERO

EVIL HAT PRODUCTIONS

 3-5 PLAYERS

 AGES 13 & UP

60 MINUTES

 LEARN TO PLAY!
evilh.at/kaiju-learn

 EVIL HAT PRODUCTIONS

DO YOU LOVE KAIJU?

Of course you do! Now you can own a piece of one with these fine kaiju-derivative products, available while supplies last.*

KAIJUMOJO™ MALE ENHANCEMENT PILLS

Does your beach bod need a boost? Wow ladies and gents alike with your monstrously enhanced physique!

KAIJU MUCUS MOUSSE

It's the gel that'll make your hair stand up and yell! Now in brand new non-corrosive varieties!

KAIJU MUSK COLOGNE

It's the designer scent that says go big or go home!

Make your McMansion into a McMonster with these home and garden improvement options, shipped straight to your door in our patented shielded containment units!

MASER-POWERED LAWNMOWER

When Kudzus takes over your lawn with its horrible, sentient vines, you'll be the only one on the block with the hardware tough enough to mow them down to size!

SURPLUS DEPLETED URANIUM SIDING

We can't all be a batteboto ace pilot, but we CAN own a piece of almost entirely unradioactive slag left over from our most recent cleanup operations. A sure-fire way to both protect your home AND sterilize your pets!

KAIJUDOO™ FERTILIZER

Let's face it, the only way you'll ever beat Becky McPherson's prize-winning watermelon is to go big—big like a 500-foot-tall fire-breathing, skyscraper-stomping death-lizard! After you use our patented, entirely nonsentient KaijuDoo™ soil enhancement product, Becky won't even come close to touching your melons!

Turn your foodie into a kaijoodie with these can't-find-anywhere-else delicacies, grown in an undisclosed location using our very own insulated vat system!

KAIJUMILK™ NON-DAIRY CREAMER

Regular old triple-caffeine espresso not doing the job for you like it used to? Just a few drops of our creamer added to your coffee will lighten your step and NOT cause you to combust!

ANTIOXIDANT KAIJUBERRIES

Just one berry, delivered very, very carefully to your door, can provide enough antioxidants to last you for a whole year. You can't prove otherwise!

FARM-FRESH KAIJUFISH FILLETS

Yes, it IS food.
Yes you CAN eat it.
Yes that strange growth IS completely normal!

Giant footprints got you down? Not feeling safe? No worries! Our military technology division has produced these consumer-friendly versions of our deadliest weapons!

OPEN-CARRY BATTEBOT JUNIOR™

Tired of the Aces getting all the glory? Get this scaled-down-for-home-use version of the same armaments that go toe to toe with kaiju! (Do not go toe to toe with a kaiju, like seriously.)

ADOLESCENT NINJA AMPHIBIANS

These non-infringing uplifted supersoldiers will be yours to command! Completely necessary (or they'll kill you) lily pond not included with purchase.

GENE THERAPY

Why carry an arsenal when you can BE the arsenal? Okay, why not ALSO be the arsenal? Our "instamutant" gene therapies are totally legal or at least the FDA hasn't told us they aren't yet!

KAIJU NAME

KAIJU SKILLS   **DANGER ASPECTS**

+ ☐ **CASUALTY**

+ ☐ **DESTRUCTION**

+ ☐ **TERROR**

KAIJU NAME

KAIJU SKILLS   **DANGER ASPECTS**

+ ☐ **CASUALTY**

+ ☐ **DESTRUCTION**

+ ☐ **TERROR**

KAIJU NAME

KAIJU SKILLS   **DANGER ASPECTS**

+ ☐ **CASUALTY**

+ ☐ **DESTRUCTION**

+ ☐ **TERROR**

KAIJU NAME

KAIJU SKILLS   **DANGER ASPECTS**

+ ☐ **CASUALTY**

+ ☐ **DESTRUCTION**

+ ☐ **TERROR**

EMPLOYEE RECORD

ASPECTS
HIGH CONCEPT

INTERVIEW

ADDITIONAL

MODES & SKILLS

GOOD (+3) MODE	FAIR (+2) MODE	AVERAGE (+1) MODE
SKILL FOC. SPEC.	SKILL FOC. SPEC.	SKILL FOC. SPEC.

STUNTS

STRESS ☐1☐ ☐2☐ ☐3☐ ☐4☐ & CONSEQUENCES
MILD (2)

MODERATE (4)

SEVERE (6)